Cybersecurity for Hospitals and Healthcare Facilities

A Guide to Detection and Prevention

Luis Ayala

Apress®

Cybersecurity for Hospitals and Healthcare Facilities: A Guide to Detection and Prevention

Luis Ayala
Fredericksburg, Virginia, USA

ISBN-13 (pbk): 978-1-4842-2154-9   ISBN-13 (electronic): 978-1-4842-2155-6
DOI 10.1007/978-1-4842-2155-6

Library of Congress Control Number: 2016951946

Managing Director: Welmoed Spahr
Acquisitions Editor: Susan McDermott
Developmental Editor: Laura Berendson
Technical Reviewer: Janie Gittleman
Editorial Board: Steve Anglin, Pramila Balen, Laura Berendson, Aaron Black, Louise Corrigan, Jonathan Gennick, Robert Hutchinson, Celestin Suresh John, Nikhil Karkal, James Markham, Susan McDermott, Matthew Moodie, Natalie Pao, Gwenan Spearing
Coordinating Editor: Rita Fernando
Copy Editor: Kim Burton-Weisman
Compositor: SPi Global
Indexer: SPi Global
Cover image: Designed by Freepik

Distributed to the book trade worldwide by Springer Science+Business Media New York, 233 Spring Street, 6th Floor, New York, NY 10013. Phone 1-800-SPRINGER, fax (201) 348-4505, e-mail orders-ny@springer-sbm.com, or visit www.springer.com. Apress Media, LLC is a California LLC and the sole member (owner) is Springer Science + Business Media Finance Inc (SSBM Finance Inc). SSBM Finance Inc is a Delaware corporation.

For information on translations, please e-mail rights@apress.com, or visit www.apress.com.

Apress and friends of ED books may be purchased in bulk for academic, corporate, or promotional use. eBook versions and licenses are also available for most titles. For more information, reference our Special Bulk Sales–eBook Licensing web page at www.apress.com/bulk-sales.

Any source code or other supplementary materials referenced by the author in this text is available to readers at www.apress.com. For detailed information about how to locate your book's source code, go to www.apress.com/source-code/.

Printed on acid-free paper

I want to thank my wife, Paula, who has been with me through thick and thin for the last 35 years. I also want to thank our son, Christopher.

Contents at a Glance

Contents

About the Author

Luis Ayala worked for the US Department of Defense for more than 25 years, with the past 11 years at the Defense Intelligence Agency. Prior to his appointment as a defense intelligence senior leader in 2008, he held several leadership positions at the branch and division levels.

His tenure culminated with the position as senior technical expert (facilities/construction). Mr. Ayala earned his Bachelor of Architecture degree from Pratt Institute and he received his Master of Science and Technology Intelligence from the National Intelligence University. NIU is the intelligence community's sole accredited, federal degree granting institution. His master's thesis, titled "Cybersecure Facilities for the Intelligence Community," is classified. Mr. Ayala was awarded the DIA Civilian Expeditionary Medal and the Civilian Combat Support Medal.

Mr. Ayala is the author of the *Cybersecurity Lexicon* (Apress, 2016) and *Cyber-Physical Attack Recovery Procedures* (Apress, 2016). He provides independent consulting services in cybersecurity for hospitals and building controls, and in cyber-physical attack recovery planning, including discrete penetration testing and vulnerability analysis.

About the Technical Reviewer

Janie Gittleman, PhD, MRP, is currently chief of the Facilities and Operations Division and Occupational Safety, Health & Environmental Compliance (FAC-3A) Mission Services, Office of Facilities and Services, at the Defense Intelligence Agency. Previously, Dr. Gittleman was associate director for safety and health research at the Center to Protect Workers' Rights (CPWR)—Center for Construction Research and Training (the National Construction Center funded by the National Institute for Occupational Safety and Health [NIOSH]). There she oversaw and conducted intra- and extramural research on construction safety and health for a decade.

Prior to her work at CPWR, she served as a NIOSH-based public health officer and senior scientist for the Office for the Secretary of Health during the September 11, 2001, and anthrax events. There she developed and reviewed state-based proposals for bioterrorism resources and developed benchmarks for evaluation the use of funds. While at NIOSH, she also served as chief of the Hearing Loss Prevention and Surveillance Branches at the NIOSH Pittsburgh Research Laboratory.

Early in her career, Dr. Gittleman conducted health hazard evaluations nationwide and participated in the Epidemic Intelligence Service (EIS) program of the Centers for Disease Control and Prevention (CDC). As an EIS officer, she oversaw and managed the Adult Blood Lead Epidemiology and Surveillance Program, tracking adult lead exposures both in the United States and abroad. Her most recent funded research and publications have been focused on safety climate, performance metrics, and fall prevention.

Dr. Gittleman serves on numerous national committees and workgroups, including the Science Board of the American Public Health Association, Bureau of Labor Statistics' Data Advisory Group, and the National Occupational Research Agenda (NORA) Construction Sector Council. She is a reviewer for journals in the field of occupational safety and health research and chairs numerous CDC grant review committees. She received her masters of regional planning degree in health planning and a PhD in occupational epidemiology from Cornell University.

Preface

According to an IBM report, cyber-attacks in general are on the rise and the global IT threat landscape has shifted from cyber-crime to smaller, stealthier customized attacks on government, financial services, manufacturing and healthcare industries. IBM's Security Intelligence team reports there were 237 million cyber incidents in 2006 and 108 million of those were reconnaissance attacks to discover devices, software, or vulnerabilities. Healthcare was hit with more than 17 million cyber-attacks that year.[1] That was ten years ago and the problem has only gotten worse.

Targets include utility companies, water purification facilities, dams, transportation systems, and now—hospitals. The majority of healthcare cyber-attacks have been to steal patient information or encrypt those files for ransom. The evolution of cybercrime is pointing toward cyber-attacks targeting patient health and active medical devices connected to the Internet. If there is any doubt in your mind that anyone would want to attack a hospital, look at these examples of *criminal hackers* and *terrorists*.

Hospitals around the country have been forced to pay hefty sums to criminal hackers using ransomware. Ransomware is a type of virus that restricts access to the infected computer system or networked medical device, and demands that the hospital pay a ransom to the malware operators to remove the restriction.[2] According to Kevin Haley, Director of Symantec Security Response, there was an average of 1,000 ransomware attacks per day in 2015. In 2016, there have been days where that number has reached 4,000. Very few of them are attacks against hospitals, but that could change as hackers eye bigger and bigger ransoms. "Everybody is running from whatever they were doing to this," Haley said, "because the dollars are big, the risk is low, and it's easy to get into."

On June 11, 2011, a prominent web Jihadist from the Shumukh al-Islam forum, Yaman Mukhaddab, launched a campaign to recruit male and female volunteers for a new electronic Jihad group. The campaign begins with a clear definition of the group's tasks and priorities. Mukhaddab says, "Simply put, it is a cyber-terror base, for launching electronic terror attacks on major infidel powers, specifically the U.S., the U.K., and France, no others. This base is not going to attack, for instance, the sites of Shi'a, Christians, apostates, slanderers, liar sites and forums or anything else. I repeat: it will only target the U.S., the U.K., and France."[3]

The purpose of this book is to alert the healthcare industry of the consequences of a cyber-physical attack on active medical devices, so they will incorporate a variety of layered security approaches to make sure that those consequences don't happen.

Healthcare facilities today rely on a great many software applications running on multiple computer networks to do everything from storing patient medical histories to turning the lights off when an employee leaves the building for the day. Hospitals cannot run efficiently without computers. Some medical device networks communicate wirelessly, while others are cabled directly to the "backbone," and every patient room in the hospital has an Ethernet connection that anyone can plug into.

---

[1] https://www-03.ibm.com/press/us/en/pressrelease/7815.wss
[2] Keith Wagstaff, "Big Paydays Force Hospitals to Prepare for Ransomware Attacks," NBC News, April 23, 2016.
[3] Gilad Zahavi, "SenseCy 2014 Annual Cyber Intelligence Report," SenseCy Blog, https://blog.sensecy.com/tag/cyber-terror/, January 15, 2015.

In this book, I describe ways hackers can attack hospital data networks, medical device data systems, and a hospital's building controls system. Each in its own way is vital to hospital operations, and sometimes these networks are linked to each other. A cyber-attack on a medical device data system could interfere with the transfer of diagnostic information from one medical device to another. A cyber-physical attack on a hospital building controls could shut down vital utilities (electricity, water, natural gas, oxygen, etc.) or just as easily turn up the heat—literally. Both of these types of networks have been successfully attacked recently.

The cyber-physical attacks that scare me are those we haven't seen yet and those are a cyber-physical attack that changes the operation of active medical devices (AMD) that patients rely on for their very survival. Multiple software applications as well as active medical devices run on the hospital data network (sometimes referred to as the hospital information system). Each application and every device running on that network represents a possible entry point for a cyber-physical attack. So, for example the software for a computerized practitioner order entry system may have hidden backdoors that would permit a hacker to gain access to the hospital data network. The backdoors may have been discovered and a security patch released, but 90 percent of security patches are never even downloaded from the vendor website.

Another thing to consider is the possibility that someone, or some foreign government will develop malevolent artificial intelligence (MAI) intended specifically to attack a nation's healthcare system.[4] MAI is potentially much more dangerous than hazardous software (HS) or hazardous intelligent software (HIS), such as a Trojan horse or milware (military grade malware), because as Nick Bostrom says in his typology of information hazards, MAI represents "computer-related risks in which the threat would derive primarily from the cognitive sophistication of the program rather than the specific properties of any actuators to which the system initially has access."[5]

As I was finishing this book, I was asked why I did not include a discussion on the vulnerabilities of remote patient monitoring networks (RPMN) and medical body area networks (MBAN). Two reasons. First, I wanted to get this book out as soon as possible to alert the healthcare industry to the very real possibility of cyber-physical attacks against active medical devices and passive medical devices (PMD) and the hospital building itself. Second, RPMNs and MBANs are unique and fairly recent technologies that are evolving rapidly, so they require a great deal of research.

I am not a lawyer and this is not legal advice, but it seems to me that most hospitals are just a few clicks away from a multi-million-dollar due care/due diligence lawsuit. The terms look similar; however, there is a subtle difference that can create a "double whammy" in fines. *Due diligence* is when the hospital takes the effort to conduct a "reasonable examination of the security systems" within a building, campus, and so forth. *Due care* is when the hospital actually executes a strategy to protect and prevent the medical equipment and building's controls system from being affected.

A "reasonable examination of the security systems" is "usually" defined by what a similar person or organization would do in the same situation. If hospital management neglects to educate themselves on the security flaws of networked active medical devices or building automation controls, this could be considered a due diligence issue. This becomes especially concerning if previously it was disclosed that the network, active medical devices or building controls system had security flaws.

Due care is also based around "reasonable action." If a building owner has a small strip mall it is not reasonable for someone to expect him to put the building controls interface in a steel reinforced room with armed security. However, if he is in charge of a Federal Reserve Bank, that level of security may be considered reasonable. Depending on the severity (loss of life or property), I believe after a cyber-physical attack some lawyers will argue that the hospital should be held liable for the attacker's actions.

---

[4] Federico Pistono and Roman V. Yampolskiy, "Unethical Research: How to Create a Malevolent Artificial Intelligence," University of Louisville, May 2016.

[5] Nick Bostrom, "Information Hazards: A Typology of Potential Harms From Knowledge," *Review of Contemporary Philosophy*, (10) 2011.

Introduction

I began this project simply to determine how vulnerable hospital and healthcare building equipment is to cyber-physical attack in the hopes I could develop recommendations on how to protect these buildings. I quickly learned that the vulnerability of the active medical devices inside the hospital to cyber-physical attacks far eclipsed that of the building equipment. A cyber-physical attack on building equipment pales in comparison to the damage a determined hacker can do if he gains access to active medical devices.[6] A hospital network controls the diagnostic, treatment and life support equipment on which patient lives depend. According to Daniel Nigrin, chief information officer of Boston Children's Hospital, "These attacks can do a lot more than get your data; they can really disrupt the day-to-day operations of your facilities."[7]

It seems that just about every day we are learning about new and creative ways in which a healthcare facility can be attacked by determined hackers. This is not a how-to book. In this book, I show what hackers can do, why hackers would target a hospital, the way they research a target, ways that hackers can gain access to active medical devices (cyber-attack vectors), how hackers hope to monetize their cyber-attack, and hopefully convince hospital administrators to take action now—before their hospital becomes the next victim.

Active medical devices require wireless communication and Internet connectivity for software-based control of therapies and network-based transmission of patients' stored medical information.[8] This combination makes active medical devices more vulnerable to cyber-physical attack. According to a recent study, the Field Security Office in the Office of Information Security at the Veterans Administration (VA) collects statistics on the prevalence of malicious software infections within its 156 medical centers. Between January 2009 and December 2011, the VA detected 142 separate instances of malware infections affecting 207 medical devices found in radiation oncology, radiology, clinical lab, GI lab, ophthalmology imaging, cardiology imaging, pharmacy, sleep lab, cardiac catheterization lab, pulmonary, dental, audiology, dictation, and neurology.[9] A common outcome was the unavailability of care because of computer outages. In one extreme instance, a computer virus infection in a catheterization lab required transport of patients to a different hospital.

In the fall of 2013, the Mayo Clinic asked a team of white hat hackers to try and hack 40 different active medical devices to see which ones were vulnerable to cyber-attack. After a week looking for backdoors into magnetic resonance imaging scanners, ultrasound equipment, ventilators, electroconvulsive therapy machines, and dozens of other contraptions, the team reported that every device had vulnerabilities ranging from defenseless operating systems to generic passwords that couldn't be changed. They reported that an infusion pump, for example could be controlled remotely by a malicious hacker to cause the machine to

---

[6]Monte Reel and Jordan Roberson, "It's Way Too Easy to Hack the Hospital," Bloomberg, November 2015.
[7]Carolyn Johnson and Matt Zapotosky, "Under pressure to digitize everything, hospitals are hackers' biggest new target," *Washington Post*, April 1, 2016.
[8]Kramer, Baker, Ransford, Molina-Markham, Stewart, Fu, Reynolds, "Security and Privacy Qualities of Medical Devices: An Analysis of FDA Postmarket Surveillance," PLOS One, July 19, 2012.
[9]Kramer, Baker, Ransford, Molina-Markham, Stewart, Fu, Reynolds, "Security and Privacy Qualities of Medical Devices: An Analysis of FDA Postmarket Surveillance," PLOS One, July 19, 2012.

dump an entire vial of medication into a patient, but a hospital staff member keeping an eye on the pump from a centralized monitoring station wouldn't notice a thing.

In another example, security researchers used "honeypots" (fake machines mimicking real equipment), to lure a hacker to attack the machines. There were more than 55,000 successful logins, 24 successful exploits, and 299 malware payloads.[10] The top-three hacker source countries were Netherlands, China, and Korea.

For the past several years, hackers have been able to compromise active medical devices in a hospital such as an X-ray scanner or an infusion pump, and they typically use the machine as a permanent base from which to probe the hospital network. Their goal is to steal personally identifiable information (PII) or patient health information (PHI), and this can easily be done because hospitals are at least a decade behind the standard cybersecurity curve. A stolen credit card number sells for less than $10 on the Web's black market; patient profiles can fetch ten times as much.[11] To these hackers, it is just about resale value.

To a terrorist the motivation is not measured in dollars. It is measured in lives. Terrorists capable of immolating or decapitating a person will not hesitate to render active medical devices not just useless, but deadly. It's just a matter of time before terrorist hackers take control of hospital diagnostic, treatment and surgical machines and attempt to injure patients. I say this because as early as 2011, Jay Radcliffe, a researcher and a diabetic, appeared at the Def Con hacking conference and demonstrated how he could hack his Medtronic insulin pump, manipulating it to deliver a potentially lethal dose.

In recent news, we have read how hackers struck hospitals with ransomware that prevented staff from accessing patient records or scheduling appointments. I suspect these cyber-attacks were not targeted specifically at hospitals, but rather were malicious emails randomly sent to many thousands of computers. It just so happened that some of those computers were in hospitals and the resulting news frenzy implied the hospitals were targeted specifically. Now that hackers realize the value of the medical networks to the hospital staff, I believe they will begin to target the hospital's active medical devices because they see that as the goose that laid the golden egg. The Citadel virus is ransomware designed to restrict a user's access to his or her own files, and it can be used to demand payment to restore access to ransomed active medical devices.

According to a recent study by a cyber-security firm, while in the past hackers have used ransomware to compromise patient health records, the authors state that others will eventually pursue the compromise of patient health itself.[12]

Hackers have seen that hospitals are more likely to pay up without a fight because they cannot afford the downtime of restoring patient files from backups or shutting down their systems for very long.[13] Hacking active medical devices has the potential of being much more lucrative and criminal hackers will not ask for a $500 payment to unlock an MRI, PET, CT scanner, or X-ray machine image data. They will ask for much, much more. A terrorist hacker, on the other hand will not ask for money. He will simply hack active medical devices to deliver fatal doses of drugs or X-rays, or he will change pharmacological databases so drug-drug Interactions (DDI) go undetected, until it is too late for hospital staff to notice.

What's worse is hackers are convinced they will get away with extortion because unlike the physical world, in the cyber domain law enforcement is largely absent, unable to offer any meaningful deterrence or protection. Hackers are also adept at erasing forensic evidence that might reveal their identity, and leaving false trails for investigators to follow to send them in the wrong direction. In addition, intruders are often based in a foreign country making extradition once a hacker is identified very difficult.

Complicating all of this is the fact that hospitals are in the process of digitizing patient records.[14] More and more, hospitals are dependent on computerized systems to coordinate healthcare, communicate

---

[10]"68,000 Medical Machines Are Wide Open to Hackers," Komando, October 1, 2015.

[11]Monte Reel and Jordan Roberson, "It's Way Too Easy to Hack the Hospital," Bloomberg, November 2015.

[12]"Securing Hospitals: A research study and blueprint," Independent Security Evaluators, http://www.securityevaluators.com, February 23, 2016.

[13]Kalev Leetaru, "Hacking Hospitals and Holding Hostages: Cybersecurity in 2016," Forbes, March 29, 2016.

[14]Carolyn Johnson and Matt Zapotosky, "Under pressure to digitize everything, hospitals are hackers' biggest new target," Washington Post, April 1, 2016.

critical medical data, and avoid medication errors. A patient's well-being is at stake when a hacker attacks. Increasingly, doctors and nurses depend on this data to perform time-sensitive, life-saving work.

Unless hospitals and other healthcare facilities take the steps necessary now to secure their active medical devices, they will be targeted for cyber-physical attack, possibly with life-threatening consequences. Litigation is bound to follow; the resulting punitive awards will drive up hospital insurance cost, and healthcare costs in general. It is not enough for a hospital to say that they took the normal standard of care in their industry—they will be called upon to show that they took every reasonable precaution. A cyber-physical attack fatality will undoubtedly result in increased regulations for hospitals and higher costs for compliance.

The lack of attention by hospital administrators in this area is understandable because they are focused on patient care and not cyber issues they never had to deal with before. Add to that the fact that hospitals typically spend only 2 or 3 percent of their budget for IT and hospital systems often are a mish-mash of legacy analog systems and newly installed digital systems.

Cyber-Attack Vectors

This is a path or means by which a hacker can gain access to a hospital computer, a medical grade network server or expensive active medical devices in order to deliver a payload or malicious outcome. An example attack vector would be when a hacker sends a virus in an email that infects a computer at a nurses' station. The hospital's antivirus protection quickly scrubs the computer at the nurses' station, but the active medical devices aren't well guarded. A virus on a nurse's computer will quickly spread throughout the network, eventually slipping into radiological machines, blood gas analyzers, and other devices that run on antiquated operating systems, such as Windows XP or Windows 2000. Altogether, I came up with over 175 cyber-attack vectors that can be used against hospitals. The following lists some of the major cyber-attack vectors:

- *Internet access*: If your hospital is connected to the Internet, your network has already been scanned and mapped, and back doors have been installed on your network(s).

- *Wireless network*: If you use wireless active medical devices, they have already been scanned and mapped by hackers.

- *Insider threat*: Deliberate or inadvertent malicious activity, often criminal behavior.

- *Direct-access attack*: Gaining physical access to an active medical device.

- *Removable media*: USB, floppy, CD, laptop, anything that can connect directly to an active medical device or building equipment.

- *Email*: Malware delivered by phishing email such as a virus, Trojan horse or worm.

- *Other networks*: A connection to the enterprise network can be one way to get into active medical devices, although it is usually the other way around. Once a hacker gains access to a C-arm X-ray machine, he can move laterally across the network to infect other active medical devices. The C-arm X-ray machine becomes the "pivot point." This example is a tough one because mobile medical equipment may harbor a virus you already eliminated from the network. Next time it's used, the virus reinfects the network and you are left wondering how the hacker got in this time. He didn't.

- *Supply chain*: If the active medical device is made overseas, it's more likely to have some hidden software programs you didn't ask for, and don't know are there.

- *Improper installation or usage*: Deliberate or inadvertent activity.

- *Theft of equipment*: Lose a vital piece of equipment and your system can be left defenseless.

- *Cyber-drone*: A drone can monitor a hospital by hacking wireless signals such as from network printers you didn't know are there (with default passwords).

- *Other*: Whatever new ideas hackers come up with.

Cyber-Attack Surface

The sum of all the "cyber-attack vectors" is called the *attack surface*. The attack vectors can be categorized in four groups based on what they are attacking. A hacker can attack a network server, a client workstation, the network itself or the medical device. Legacy active medical devices are very difficult to defend, so IT departments focus on defending the network, servers, and client workstations. Once a virus gets on a network, every device in that enclave is at risk of compromise and active medical devices in that node can probably be manipulated directly to accept malicious commands.

Let me point out right now that in order for a hacker to compromise an active medical device he would need a great deal of technical training in the fields of electrical, mechanical and biomedical engineering, computer science, significant medical training, and probably an extensive background in pharmacology. In short, a successful cyber-physical attack against a complex active medical device is remote and we may be several years away from a terrorist being able to pull one off. My hope when I began this project was that it would be nearly impossible. Sad to say, that is not the case. I believe it can be done, but probably not by a single individual. However, a well-funded criminal organization or a rogue nation-state with significant resources and talented engineers would have little difficulty in successfully attacking active medical devices in multiple target hospitals simultaneously using only the Internet.

The bad news is there are many cyber-attack vectors and a hacker only needs one to be successful. The good news is you can reduce your cyber-attack surface so when the hacker comes "rattling the doorknobs," he will see the doors are locked, and hopefully move on to the next target.

Who Are These Hackers?

You will hear security professionals say it's impossible to prevent a committed adversary from penetrating your defense, but you need to consider who the adversary could be. There are several classes of adversaries in the cyber-physical realm with varying degrees of expertise, and to make matters worse, they are evolving rapidly, continuously honing their skills.

- *Script kiddies*: Amateurs capable of downloading "canned" attack tools. Relatively unsophisticated but dangerous nonetheless, and easily defeated by an effective patch management protocol and basic cyber-hygiene.

- *Criminals*: Seasoned IT professionals capable of hacking into enterprise networks and carrying out denial of service attacks, stealing bank account information or encrypting a hard drive for ransom.

- *Terrorists*: Advanced persistent threat, not interested in denial of service attacks or Bitcoin ransom pocket change. Their goal is the use of violence, or threatened use of violence, in order to achieve a political, religious, or ideological aim.

- *Nation states*: Sophisticated advanced persistent threat probably capable of targeting specific individuals.

So far, hospitals appear to have focused on preventing indiscriminate, untargeted cyber-attacks by script kiddies and criminals and given little thought to the possibility of terrorist attacks or attacks by nation states at a time of cyberwarfare. Unfortunately, both are very real possibilities that would seriously affect healthcare in the United States. These adversaries are capable of attacks that manipulate records or active medical devices in order to fully compromise patient health.

How Do They Do It?

Control systems for building equipment and active medical devices are not typically thought of as "industrial" controls, but they operate in much the same way, although they use different protocols, ports, and services. A field device (a boiler, an MRI, or an infusion pump) is a piece of sophisticated electrical/mechanical equipment that receives commands from a programmable logic controller (a computer) and follows those commands. In a BCS, the protocol used could be Modbus, in which case the commands are called *function codes*. All function codes are defined in the Modbus standard that building equipment manufacturers adopt; however, which function codes apply to a particular device is determined by the equipment designer.

Modbus is a simple protocol with no encryption and no authentication. So, if a hacker can gain access to the hospital network, any function codes he sends to a particular device are followed without question. Of course, the network has several levels of security the hacker would need to defeat to get to an active medical device. Alternatively, an insider sometimes can merely plug a laptop into the equipment directly and install a virus.

The bad news is that all the function codes are publicly documented, so any hacker can find them readily and prepare a customized cyber-attack that injects false commands to make active medical devices operate in a way that was never intended by the designer. A malicious hacker can send commands to an active medical device to literally destroy itself.

Unfortunately, some of the tools that hackers use are capable of residing entirely in volatile memory, writing nothing to disc. The hacker need not create a new process when he is able to inject malicious software into a compromised process. This results in little forensic evidence for us to discover later. Hackers are very good at covering their tracks and sometimes leave false footprints to send us down the wrong path. They modify timestamps, delete added users, revert any modifications they make to registry keys, and clean log files.

Wireless Technology Update

Hospital Bluetooth and wireless systems operate on radio waves and certain frequencies can become clogged or can interfere with sensitive medical equipment. Visible-Light Communication (VLC) systems for transmitting data offer the promise of being faster and more secure than traditional wireless systems. A VLC is also wireless, but instead of using radio waves (that can be intercepted), a VLC transfers data using light emitting diodes (LEDs) to a receiving sensor through a series of quick flashes that are unperceivable to the human eye.

VLC systems are more secure because they limit the range of the signal by operating in an enclosed environment. That greatly reduces the ability of hackers to interfere with network traffic from outside the building. Researchers have demonstrated the ability to use VLCs to transmit data at speeds of 300 Mbps, 500 Mbps and 1.6 Gbp. Nanocrystal technology promises to boost VLC data speeds to 2 Gbp, and future VLC speed may go as high as 10 Gbp.

CHAPTER 1

■ ■ ■

Hacker Reconnaissance of a Hospital Network

Gone forever are the days when a patient was treated by a single physician. Today, a team of physicians and specialized medical technicians rely on complex medical equipment to diagnose and treat patients. This collaboration is made possible because electronic medical records (EMRs) securely store large amounts of medical and clinical information, which is exchanged electronically among healthcare entities by an industry-specific Medical-Grade Network (MGN). This medical information is susceptible to being stolen or held for ransom and malicious hackers can even take direct control of connected active and passive medical devices over the internet and injure patients.

The Health Information Technology for Economic and Clinical Health (HITECH) Act of 2009 provided financial incentives for Medicare and Medicaid providers who become "meaningful users" of EMRs. Among non-federal acute care hospitals, 76 percent were using a "basic" system by 2014. As of May 2015, more than 468,000 Medicare and Medicaid providers (87 percent) have received payments through the HITECH Act, totaling approximately $30.4 billion.[1]

As seen in Figure 1-1, as the implementation of HITECH Act expanded, so has the cost of data breaches at healthcare facilities in the United States.

---

[1]Tara O'Neill, "Are Electronic Medical Records Worth The Costs Of Implementation?" American Action Forum, August 6, 2015. https://www.americanactionforum.org/research/are-electronic-medical-records-worth-the-costs-of-implementation/

Electronic supplementary material The online version of this chapter (doi:10.1007/978-1-4842-2155-6_1) contains supplementary material, which is available to authorized users.

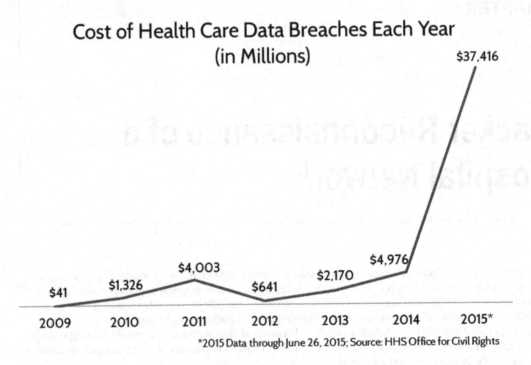

Figure 1-1. *Rising cost of healthcare data breaches since 2009*

The MGN is made up of three layers: the networked infrastructure layer, the interactive services layer, and the application layer. The network infrastructure that the MGN runs on is also used by the business enterprise. Also, it controls the functions or parameters of connected *active medical devices* (AMD) and *passive medical devices* (PMD).

An AMD interfaces directly with a patient to administer medical treatment. A PMD monitors patient health, and although not used to administer treatment, a PMD can be hacked and weaponized either by a hacker silencing the alarm when the patient needs attention or sounding an alarm when emergency treatment is not needed (which could harm the patient).

The patient benefit of all this technology is the delivery of healthcare that is efficient, affordable, and until now, safe. This is where it all begins. If a hacker can successfully accomplish footprinting, scanning, enumeration, and network mapping, there is no doubt in my mind that he will gain access to your MGN, and not only steal patient information or hold the network hostage, but eventually take control of the active medical devices and jeopardize the lives of patients. Your goal is to try to stop a hacker at every step, and to do that, you have to know the process that hackers go through.

Footprinting

Footprinting is how the hacker starts his analysis of the target hospital network.[2] The hacker sifts through open source material found on the Internet to learn all he can about the hospital, including who works there, which equipment is used there, and where the equipment is located. A hacker may visit the hospital, sniff the wireless spectrum, look in dumpsters, and use social engineering to assemble a very good picture of the hospital and its active medical devices to determine where the vulnerabilities are.

---

[2] I use the terms "hospital" and "healthcare facility" interchangeably because to me it is merely a matter of scale. Because healthcare facilities don't have a large IT department, they are attacked more frequently than large hospitals. However, attack prevention, defense, and recovery processes are similar.

Once the hacker knows who manufactured the device that he intends to attack, he finds a copy of the operating and maintenance manuals (many are available online). Unfortunately, those manuals usually reveal the *default password* set at the factory. To make matters worse, *some manufacturers recommend that the healthcare facility keep the default password*, because this makes it easier for the manufacturer's technician to test the equipment or perform maintenance. This same glaring vulnerability makes hacking the device simple.

■ **Caution**   *Change the default passwords on all of your medical devices—now.*

The hacker launches an **account-harvesting attack** to collect all the user account names on a computer network. Account harvesting involves using computer programs to search areas on the Internet to gather lists of email addresses from a number of sources, including chatrooms, domain names, instant message users, message boards, newsgroups, online directories for web pages belonging to professional societies, medical web pages, and other online destinations. A sophisticated hacker uses **data mining** to analyze a vast amount of information about a target hospital.

Many hackers resort to **social engineering attacks.** Social engineering is the art and science of getting people to do something that you want that they might not do in a normal course of action. In addition to collecting information by technical means, hackers apply various methods of social engineering, such as impersonating individuals on the telephone or other persuasive means (e.g., tricking, convincing, inducing, enticing, or provoking) to encourage someone to disclose valuable information.

Attackers look for information about who the target does business with: suppliers and customers. And they are particularly interested in IT support staff. They gather this information to better understand staff roles and responsibilities. They may use this information to pose as someone from one of their suppliers or vendors. Attackers look for information, such as birthdays, who was recently promoted, or who just had a baby. Hackers do not discount any information that they uncover. They even use bad relationships between the IT department and other offices as a wedge to gain information.

Attackers send friend requests to hospital staff on Facebook, Match.com, LinkedIn, and any other Internet sites where people divulge personal information. Staff should never give away their GPS position, or location links, or send updates divulging where they will be on vacation. When asked, instead of saying "I'm going on vacation for two weeks," I usually say, "I'm having a staycation and plan to sit at home cleaning my guns."

Hackers often use **behavior-monitoring hacks.** This involves observing the activities of hospital staff, MGN data traffic, and processes; and measuring activities against hospital policies and rules, baselines of normal activity, thresholds, and trends. Hackers have been known to resort to **shoulder surfing**, or using direct observation techniques, such as looking over a nurse's shoulder to obtain personal access information (e.g., passwords, PINs, and security codes).

The hacker is not above **dumpster diving** to obtain passwords and the hospital's directories by searching through discarded trash bins (also referred to as *skipping*). **Eavesdropping** is a low-tech technique that hackers use to listen in to a private conversation to acquire information that can provide access to an MGN. A hacker may go so far as to install a **screen scraper** virus or physical device that logs and captures information sent to a hospital staffer's computer display.

If a hacker cannot physically visit the hospital, he could use PlaceRaider to create a virtual layout of the hospital's interior. This is a novel Trojan horse visual malware app surreptitiously installed on a staffer's smartphone. It allows a hacker to engage in remote reconnaissance to obtain geolocation data and enlist its accelerometer to create a 3D map of the phone's surroundings. A hacker can download images of the physical space, study the environment, and carefully construct a three-dimensional model of indoor environments to survey the staffer's private home or workplace. PlaceRaider can be used to photograph virtual objects in the environment, such as financial documents, information on computer monitors, and personally identifiable patient information.

Scanning

After hackers research the target hospital using open source websites, such as vendor marketing materials, awarded contracts, medical conference attendee lists, and LinkedIn and Facebook pages, the hacker searches the Shodan database of devices, which are accessible over the Internet. The Shodan database allows a hacker to find IP addresses and begin port scanning to identify which operating systems the hospital uses and then figure out how to access the hospital's networks. If the target hospital is accessible by Shodan (it should not be), Shodan reveals all services running on the hospital's computers, and allows hackers to share this information with others (see Figures 1-2 and 1-3).

Figure 1-2. *Shodan website*

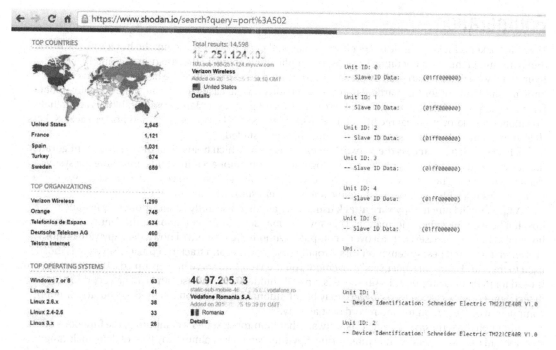

Figure 1-3. *Shodan results screen*

Other common network-discovery hacking tools include the Google Hacking Diggity Project, Nmap, Snort, Kismet, Nessus, McAfee, Sophia, and Bandolier.

Once the hacker knows which software applications are running on the target hospital's network, he can develop a specific set of tools to exploit known vulnerabilities. For example, let's say that the hacker learns that the building controls system at the target hospital is running Siemens SIMATIC STEP 7 TIA (Portal). In February 2015, Siemens reported two vulnerabilities on that software. One vulnerability allows a successful, remote man-in-the-middle attack. The other allows a hacker with local access to reconstruct protection-level passwords. Although a Siemens software update is available, it is likely that it hasn't been installed in many hospitals.

A hacker will probably launch an **address space probe attack** when he finds your hospital networks on the Shodan website and locates your IP address space. The hacker is looking for security holes that might be exploited on the hospital's network, such as unpatched vulnerabilities.

A hacker uses a passive technique called **network sniffing** to monitor hospital network communication, decode protocols, and examine headers and network traffic for information of interest. It is both a review technique and a target identification and analysis technique. The hacker may launch a **probing attack** to attempt to connect to well-known services that may be running on the hospital network to see which operating system exists and potentially identify the version of software that it is running. A smart hacker will attempt a few common username and password combinations on several computers, resulting in failed login attempts. This is called a **doorknob-rattling attack** and can go undetected, unless the data related to login failures from all the hosts is collected and aggregated to check for doorknob rattling from any remote destination.

If the hacker is really ambitious, he may resort to **emanations analysis**, or obtaining data by monitoring and resolving electronic signals emitted by medical equipment that contains the data, but is not designed to communicate the data.

Enumeration

Now the hacker is looking a little deeper into the hospital networks. By this point, he has found the servers and determined the exact operating systems, the applications software that are running, and he has figured out who the users are—all by passively monitoring network traffic. The hacker also finds a list of known vulnerabilities for that particular network version and can easily determine if the software updates have been applied. Unfortunately, only about 10 percent of patches for known vulnerabilities are actually downloaded, so knowing what the hospital network consists of is key to gaining unauthorized access. Less than 10 percent of downloaded security patches are ever installed.

A hacker will try to **access the network's config.bog file**, which holds all of the system's configuration data as well as usernames and passwords for logging in to operator accounts and controlling the systems managed by them. This allows the hacker to overwrite files on the device to get root access on a system (a Windows system with a Java virtual machine and the client software running on it).

A hacker will launch a **spyware attack** using software that is secretly or surreptitiously installed on a hospital network to gather information. That spyware may send information to another entity without the hospital's consent, or assert control over a computer without the hospital's knowledge. Spyware is mostly classified into four types: system monitors, Trojan horse, adware, and tracking cookies. Spyware is mostly used to track and store Internet users' movements on the Web, and serve up pop-up ads. Whenever spyware is used for malicious purposes, its presence is typically hidden from the user and can be very difficult to detect. Some spyware, such as *keyloggers*, may be intentionally installed on a shared, corporate, or public computer in order to monitor and record user activity.

Although the term *spyware* suggests software that monitors a staffer's computing, the functions of spyware can extend beyond simple monitoring. Spyware can collect almost any type of data, including personal information, such as Internet surfing habits, user logins, and bank or credit account information. Spyware can also interfere with a user's control of a computer by installing additional software or redirecting web browsers. Some spyware can change computer settings, which results in slow Internet connection speed, unauthorized changes in browser settings, or changes to other software settings. Spyware does not necessarily spread in the same way as a virus or worm, because infected systems generally do not attempt to transmit or copy the software to other computers.

■ **Note**   Some spyware cannot be completely removed.

Common spyware programs illustrate the diversity of behaviors found in these attacks. Note that, like computer viruses, researchers give names to spyware programs, which is not likely used by the virus creators. Programs may be grouped into "families" based not on shared program code, but on common behaviors, or by "following the money" of apparent financial or business connections. Programs that are frequently installed together may be described as parts of the same spyware package, even if they function separately. The following are some examples:

- **CoolWebSearch** is a group of programs that takes advantage of Internet Explorer vulnerabilities. The package directs traffic to advertisements on websites, including CoolWebSearch.com. It displays pop-up ads, rewrites search engine results, and alters the infected computer's hosts file to direct Domain Name System (DNS) lookups to these sites.

- **HuntBar** is also known as WinTools or Adware. Websearch is installed by an ActiveX drive-by download at affiliate websites, or by advertisements displayed by other spyware programs—an example of how spyware can install more spyware. These programs add toolbars to Internet Explorer, track aggregate browsing behavior, redirect affiliate references, and display advertisements.

- **Internet Optimizer**, also known as DyFuCa, redirects Internet Explorer error pages to advertising. When users follow a broken link or enter an erroneous URL, they see a page of advertisements. However, because password-protected websites use the same mechanism as HTTP errors, Internet Optimizer makes it impossible for the user to access password-protected sites.

- Spyware such as **Look2Me** hides inside system-critical processes and starts up even in safe mode. With no process to terminate, they are harder to detect and remove, which is a combination of both spyware and a rootkit. Rootkit technology is also experiencing increased use, as newer spyware programs also have specific countermeasures against well-known anti-malware products and may prevent them from running or being installed, or even from uninstalling them.

- **Movieland**, also known as Moviepass.tv and Popcorn.net, is a movie download service that has been the subject of thousands of complaints to the Federal Trade Commission (FTC) and other agencies.

- **WeatherStudio** has a plug-in that displays a window panel near the bottom of a browser window.

- **Zango** transmits detailed information to advertisers about the websites that users visit. It also alters HTTP requests for affiliate advertisements linked from a website, so that the advertisements make unearned profit for the company. It opens pop-up ads that cover over the websites of competing companies.

- **Zlob** Trojan, or just Zlob, downloads itself to a computer via an ActiveX codec and reports information back to a control server. Information collected includes search history, websites visited, and keystrokes. More recently, Zlob has been known to hijack routers set at defaults.

Hackers are increasingly using **spy-phishing** techniques that capitalize on the trend of "blended threats." This is a hostile action to spread malicious code via multiple methods. For example, sending a malicious URL by email, with text that encourages the recipient to click the link, is a **blended threat attack**. Defined as *crimeware*, spy-phishing borrows techniques from both phishing and spyware. The downloaded applications sit silently on the user's system until the targeted URL is visited, wherein it activates, and sends information to the malicious third party. Through the use of spyware and other Trojans, spy-phishing attempts to prolong the initial phishing attack beyond the point at which the phishing site is available.

Network Mapping

By this point, the hacker can draw a very detailed layout of the hospital's network and visualize the total network environment. The hacker's network map is probably more current than your copy because he has found what's actually there. Your network map only shows what you *think* is there. The hacker's network map shows the rogue devices that employees misconfigured and those installed by equipment vendors without authorization so that they can monitor their equipment remotely. Any of these are easily hacked and used as *pivot points* for the hacker to move laterally across the hospital network (see Figure 1-4).

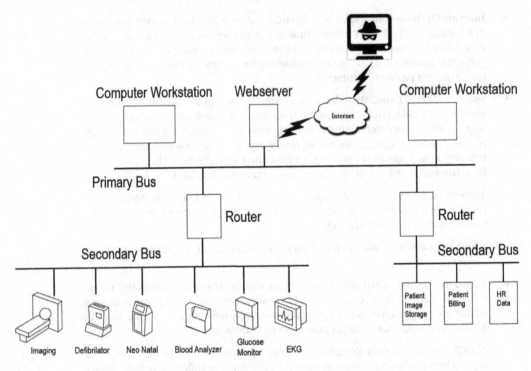

Figure 1-4. Oversimplified network map—the point is that everything's connected

Cyber-Threat Actors

I'm sure many are wondering who would want to hack a hospital or active medical devices. In the world of cybersecurity, cyber-threat actors fall into the following four general categories:

- **Hacktivists**: Such as Anonymous-affiliated groups around the world.

- **Cyber-terrorists**: The cyber units of Hezbollah and al-Qaeda (AQ), for example.

- **Cyber-criminals**: Such as groups based in the Ukraine, Eastern Europe, China, and Latin America.

- **Governments**: State-sponsored groups such as the Chinese PLA Unit 61398, also known as APT1, or the Iranian hacker groups the Izz ad-Din al-Qassam Cyber Fighters and Parastoo, which launched Operation Ababil several years ago against the U.S. financial sector.

On June 11, 2011, Yaman Mukhaddab, a prominent web Jihadist from the Shumukh al-Islam forum, launched a campaign to recruit male and female volunteers for a new Electronic Jihad group. The campaign began with a clear definition of the group's tasks and priorities. Mukhaddab said, "Simply put, it is a cyber-terror base for launching electronic terror attacks on major infidel powers, specifically the U.S., the U.K., and France, no others. This base is not going to attack, for instance, the sites of Shi'a, Christians, apostates, slanderers, liar sites and forums, or anything else. I repeat: it will only target the U.S., the U.K., and France."[3]

---

[3]Gilad Zahavi, "SenseCy 2014 Annual Cyber Intelligence Report," SenseCy Blog. Last accessed January 15, 2015. https://blog.sensecy.com/tag/cyber-terror/

■ ■ ■

CHAPTER 2

How Hackers Gain Access to a Healthcare Facility or Hospital Network

This is where the hacker begins to exploit the hospital's network. The hacker gains access to an active medical device on a hospital network in any one of dozens of ways. Having successfully carried out a spear-phishing campaign, the hacker knows who the network administrator is, who the technicians are, and has even obtained some email addresses for hospital staff from attendee lists at medical conferences posted to the Internet. Hospital directories are also a good source of information. When an unsuspecting hospital employee opens an email claiming to be from a bank, the IRS, hospital HR, or from a spoofed name of a friend, the malicious payload is delivered. Fully 78 percent of phishing emails will impersonate hospital IT department or anti-virus vendor, and 72 percent of victim-specific phishes are sent on weekdays.

Historically, ordinary cyber-attacks were often undetectable and untraceable. A cyber-physical attack on a hospital building or on active medical devices, on the other hand, is difficult to hide because equipment is failing in real time.

Phishing Attack

Hackers rely heavily on **phishing attack**s to trick hospital staff into disclosing sensitive personal information by claiming to be a trustworthy entity in an electronic communication (e.g., Internet websites). Phishing is a digital form of social engineering that uses authentic-looking—but bogus—emails to request information from users, or directs them to a fake website that requests information. **Spear phishing** refers to targeting specific hospital staffers, luring them into opening an email that appears to come from someone they know, which infects hospital computers when they fall for the bait. **Whaling** is when a hacker uses spear phishing to target hospital administrators or other high-level hospital staff. According to security expert Rodney Joffe, "The most common vector for corporation compromise over the last three to five years has been through the use of social engineering of some kind."[1]

Another approach a hacker will take is a **vishing attack**. This is a type of phishing attack that uses a telephone ("v" is for voice) to obtain personal information. The hospital staffer is called directly by a hacker on the telephone or receives an email asking the target to call a specific phone number. Attackers usually have a recorded message that tells users to call a toll-free number and use caller ID spoofing to make it look like calls are coming from a legitimate or known phone number. The caller is then asked to punch in a credit card number or other personal information.

---

[1]Davey Winder. "Phish Your Own Staff: Arming Employees to Beat Modern Attacks," *Infosecurity*, Nov. 28, 2014.

© Luis Ayala 2016
L. Ayala, *Cybersecurity for Hospitals and Healthcare Facilities*, DOI 10.1007/978-1-4842-2155-6_2

Email Phishing Attack

Email is the preferred method of gaining access to any network that has Internet access. A hacker will send an email containing **active content** (carries out or triggers actions automatically without the intervention of a user), such as a **Remote Access Trojan** (RAT), to a hospital employee, such as a biomedical equipment technician (BMET) or a building maintenance technician. According to a 2015 data breach investigations report, 23 percent of recipients of phishing emails open them and 11 percent click an attachment.[2] Typically, doctors, nurses, and building maintenance personnel access their email using the only workstation on their desk. I recommend that hospitals increase awareness of the importance of not opening suspicious emails. Table 2-1 lists some email do's and don'ts.

Table 2-1. *Cyber-Hygiene Email Do's and Don'ts*

Do's	Don'ts
Don't open suspicious emails.	Don't use a preview pane for email, use plain text only.
Don't click links to websites in any emails.	Don't respond to email that demands that you update information and gives a link to click.
Don't respond to emails that threaten dire consequences.	Don't open email from strangers.
Always look for digital signatures.	Scan all attachments.

Chapter 8 lists examples of phrases commonly used in phishing emails. I suggest every hospital provide basic personal cyber-security training to the entire workforce. I guarantee that it will prevent some cyber-attacks.

Many companies are now initiating their own internal phishing tests to educate their workforce on the hazards of phishing. According to a company called KnowBe4, 91% of successful data breaches started with a spear-phishing attack. KnowBe4 offers a free phishing security test for up to 100 users. This test allows you to find out the percentage of users that are phish-prone. According to computer security consultant Kevin Mitnick, "Ransomware is the new way cybercriminals attack your network, but they still mostly use old-fashioned manipulation to get in."[3] Phishing is probably the most common way that they get in.

Man-in-The-Middle Attacks

A man-in-the-middle (MITM) attack is an attack where the hacker secretly relays and possibly alters the communication between two parties who believe they are directly communicating with each other. This can be very straightforward. For example, a hacker within reception range of an unencrypted Wi-Fi wireless access point can insert himself as a man-in-the-middle.

A man-in-the-middle attack performed on a building controls system (BCS) protocol modifies packets in transit, provides a spoof on the operator's computer monitor, and takes full control of the BCS. Sometimes a smart operator will very briefly notice a **voodoo mouse** (mouse cursor moves all by itself), indicating that someone else is at the controls. The hacker then inserts targeted commands capable of damaging equipment and injuring patients.

---

[2]http://www.verizonenterprise.com/DBIR/2015/
[3]https://www.knowbe4.com/what-is-cryptolocker-ransomware/

An **address resolution protocol** (**ARP**) man-in-the-middle attack is a popular method to gain access to the network flow of information on a target system. By attacking the network ARP cache tables of the controller and the workstation machines, and using the compromised computer on the control network, an adversary can route all the traffic through specific hardware (the adversary's machine). In this way, the adversary inserts their machine between a target machine and a device.

Once an adversary inserts a machine into the network data stream, he has full control and can carry out several types of attacks. One possible attack is the **replay attack**. Captured data reflecting normal operations is modified and then played back to the operator as required. The data stream appears normal and the cyber-attack goes unobserved.

Another attack method is to send false messages to the operator. This is known as **spoofing**. This may cause the operator to take an action, such as flip a circuit breaker, or it may cause the operator to think everything is fine and not take action when action is required. A command can be sent to the operator indicating a problem and when the operator follows normal procedures to correct the problem, *the operator's action actually causes* the damage to the equipment.

There are techniques to defend against man-in-the-middle attacks through port security, static tables, encryption, authentication, monitoring, and smart cards. Port security locks a specific MAC address[4] to a specific port on a managed switch and reduces the number of computers a remote adversary can access. Statically coding ARP tables on each computer prevents an adversary from changing them. Encrypting communications between devices also makes it nearly impossible to perform man-in-the-middle attacks. Protocols with strong authentication provide resilience to man-in-the-middle attacks. Monitoring for ARP poisoning adds a layer of defense. Smart cards can provide additional functionality and enhance software-only solutions, such as password authentication, by offering an additional authentication factor.

Notable man-in-the-middle tools and techniques include the following:

- **DSniff**: Dsniff, filesnarf, mailsnarf, msgsnarf, urlsnarf ,and webspy are password sniffing and network traffic analysis tools used to parse application protocols and extract information passively (passwords, email, files, etc.).

- **Fiddler2 HTTP(S)**: Fiddler captures HTTP and HTTPS traffic and logs it for the user to review (the latter by implementing man-in-the-middle interception using self-signed certificates).

- **Opendium Iceni**: Content-control software used to perform inspection of HTTPS traffic at the gateway.

- **Subterfuge**: A framework to launch multiple MITM attacks.

- **Superfish**: Malware installed as a man-in-the-middle proxy that intercepts encrypted (SSL/TLS) connections.

- **Forcepoint**: A software application, computer appliance, or cloud-based service operating at the transport layer as a transparent proxy, or at the application layer as a web proxy that can inspect network traffic to or from the Internet.

- **wsniff:** A tool for 802.11 HTTP/HTTPS based MITM attacks.

- **Cain**: A Windows graphical user interface tool that can perform MITM attacks, along with sniffing and ARP poisoning.

- **Ettercap**: A tool for LAN-based MITM attacks capable of intercepting traffic on a network segment, capturing passwords, and conducting active eavesdropping against a number of common protocols. It can also be used for computer network protocol analysis and security auditing.

---

[4]A *media access control address* (MAC address), also called a *physical address*, of a computer is a unique identifier assigned to network interfaces for communications on the physical network segment.

- **Evil Twin Router:** A term for a rogue Wi-Fi access point that appears to be a legitimate one offered at a hotel, airport, and so forth, but actually has been set up to eavesdrop on wireless communications. Basically, a wireless version of the phishing scam. An attacker fools a wireless user into connecting a laptop or mobile phone to a tainted hotspot by posing as a legitimate provider. This type of attack may be used to steal the passwords of unsuspecting users by either snooping the communication link or by phishing.

- **AirJack:** A device driver for 802.11 raw frame injection and reception that allows traffic interception and tampering for MITM attacks.

Pharming Attack

Hackers also have been known to use pharming attacks. This is a sophisticated Man-In-The-Middle attack intended to redirect a website's traffic to another, fake site. Pharming can be conducted either by changing the hosts file on a staffer's computer or by exploitation of a vulnerability in DNS server software. DNS servers are computers responsible for resolving Internet names into their real IP addresses. Compromised DNS servers are sometimes referred to as *poisoned*. Pharming requires unprotected access to target a computer, such as altering a hospital staffer's home computer, rather than a hospital server.

Indirect Cyber-Attack

A hacker can use email as an **indirect cyber-attack vector** against a hospital network that is *not even connected* to the Internet. The hacker will **email a virus to a medical equipment vendor**. The vendor reads his email on the same laptop that he then connects to your hospital network to troubleshoot a problem or load the latest security patch, thereby delivering the virus. Once a hacker gets a virus loaded on one machine, he can use that as a *pivot point* to move laterally across the network to other machines. Sure, you have firewalls, but a professional hacker can get around those.[5]

Scareware

A tactic frequently used by hackers involves convincing staffers that a virus has infected their computer, and then suggesting that they download (and pay for) fake antivirus software to remove it. **Scareware** is malicious software that uses social engineering to cause shock, anxiety, or the perception of a threat in order to manipulate users into buying unwanted software. Scareware is part of a class of malicious software that includes rogue security software, ransomware and other scam software with malicious payloads, which have limited or no benefit to users, and are pushed by unethical marketing practices. Some forms of **spyware** and **adware** also use scareware tactics. Usually, the virus is entirely fictional and the software is non-functional or it can be malware itself. The hackers are looking for a response that singles out a target as gullible and easily fooled. The target's response could identify the target as an easy "mark."

Ransomware

Ransomware is a type of criminal malware (cryptoviral extortion) that restricts access to the infected computer system in some way, and demands that the hospital pay a ransom to the malware operators to remove the restriction.[6] The computer can be a server holding patient files or a computer that is built into an active medical device. Ransomware typically propagates as a Trojan, whose payload is disguised

---

[5]Kim Zetter, "It's Insanely Easy to Hack Hospital Equipment," *Wired* magazine, April 25, 2014.
[6]Connor Mannion, "Three U.S. Hospitals Hit in String of Ransomware Attacks," NBC News, March 23, 2016.

as a seemingly legitimate file. Some forms of ransomware encrypt files on the hospital computer's hard drive, which become difficult or impossible to decrypt without paying the ransom for the encryption key. Ransomware typically enters a computer through a downloaded file or a vulnerability in a network service. The program then runs a payload, which typically takes the form of a scareware program. Figure 2-1 shows an example of what the ransomware screen looks like. Looks official? It's not.

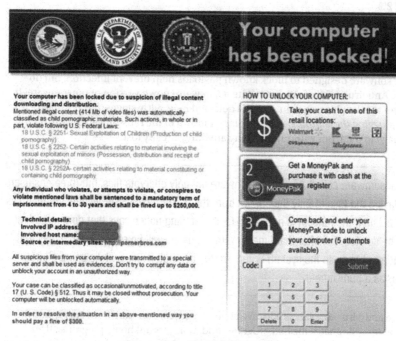

Figure 2-1. *Ransomware image via PC World.com*

According to Symantec Security, the ransomware program "Locky" spreads through spam email campaigns, many of which are disguised as invoices.[7] "Word documents containing a malicious macro are attached to these emails. If this macro is allowed to run, it will install Locky onto the victim's computer," according to Symantec. Locky has increasingly been observed infecting computers belonging to healthcare facilities and hospitals in the United States, New Zealand, and Germany.[8] A hacker may be able to encrypt image files on an active medical device as easily as they can a patient database on a server.

Some payloads are designed to lock or restrict the system until payment is made by setting the Windows Shell to itself, or even modify the master boot record and/or partition table to prevent the operating system from booting until it is repaired. Trojans such as CryptoLocker, CryptoDefense, TorrentLocker, GPCode, TROJ.RANSOM.A, Archiveus, Krotten, CryZip, Manamecrypt (CryptoHost), MayArchive, Locky, and Jigsaw utilize sophisticated encryption. Trojans that do not encrypt files include WinLock, Stamp.EK, Reveton, Citadel, Zeus, and RSA4096. Table 2-2 lists the top 10 ransomware programs by frequency.

---

[7]Connor Mannion, "Three U.S. Hospitals Hit in String of Ransomware Attacks," NBC News, March 23, 2016.
[8]US-CERT Alert (TA16-091A) Ransomware and Recent Variants Original release date: March 31, 2016. Last revised: May 6, 2016.

Table 2-2. Top 10 Ransomware Programs (Dec 2015–May 2016)[9]

Tescrypt: 42%	Crowti: 17%
FakeBsod: 15%	Brolo: 9%
Locky: 7%	Teerac: 4%
Critroni: 2%	Reveton: 2%
Cerber: 1%	Exxroute: 1%

According to Microsoft, the greatest detections in the United States were for FakeBsod, followed by Tescrypt and Brolo. Antivirus software designed to block known payloads help prevent infection, but do not protect against all attacks. Antivirus software may not detect a new unknown version of ransomware. It takes some time for encryption to take place, so if an attack is detected in its early stages, *it is possible to stop the ransomware attack by unplugging the computer*.[10] Immediate removal of the ransomware before it has completed stops further damage to data, but without salvaging anything already lost.

■ **Caution**   A new type of ransomware called Jigsaw ransomware not only encrypts files, but threatens users with a countdown. While displaying the face of Billy the Puppet from the horror movie *Saw*, victims are told files are selected by the hour for deletion if the ransom is not paid. The threatening notice says that during the first 24 hours, only a few files will be deleted, but after that time, several thousand will be removed every day that payment is missing. If users attempt to close the system or turn off the computer, Jigsaw tells users 10,000 files will be deleted on startup "as a punishment."

Webroot SecureAnywhere anti-virus software is effective at preventing ransomware from encrypting files. Webroot leaves the good files alone, eliminates the bad programs and monitors unknown programs. If an unknown program tries to exfiltrate your data while it's being monitored, it won't succeed. Keeping backups of data stored in locations inaccessible to the infected computer is highly recommended. Backups don't prevent ransomware attacks from happening, but they prevent them from having a significant impact. Ransomware that makes the computer unusable without encrypting files can be defeated by experts. A key element in making ransomware work for the attacker is a convenient untraceable payment system, such as Bitcoin.

USB Stick

A common hack to gain access to a hospital network is through a hacker at a medical trade show handing out **free USB sticks** that are infected with a virus. Use of USB sticks for exchanging information among researchers is a common practice in the medical and scientific community and at meetings. This practice should be discouraged at international meetings to avoid system corruption. When a staffer plugs the USB into a hospital computer, the virus infects the computer and then infects all other computers on the network. The beauty of this hack is that even if the network is not connected to the Internet, the virus can still get in. Once the virus is in, it can locate active medical devices, such as an MRI machine, for instance, encrypt the image files, shut it down, or threaten to cause serious damage to the MRI machine unless the hospital pays a ransom. The same is true of any other hospital device; be it a small infusion pump or a large CT scanner, it's all vulnerable. Table 2-3 lists some personal cyber-hygiene do's and don'ts for USB drives.

---

[9]https://www.microsoft.com/en-us/security/portal/mmpc/shared/ransomware.aspx
[10]Charlie Osborne, "Tick, tock: Jigsaw ransomware deletes your files as you wait," *ZDNet*, April 22, 2016.

Table 2-3. *Cyber-Hygiene USB Do's and Don'ts*

Do not use flash media unless necessary.	Scan USB drive before using.
Do not use personal USB drive on hospital PC.	Do not use hospital USB drive on non-hospital systems.
Do not download data onto removable media.	Encrypt data on USB drive when possible.
Label removable media and store safely.	Follow hospital policy to sanitize USB drive.

Hackers have even been known to infect devices that plug into a computer USB port at the factory. For example, digital picture frames that consumers plug into a computer to upload family photos contain a virus that infect the user's PC. The same can be done with any other USB device, so think twice before you plug that USB into a hospital computer, because it might be infected. If your Fitbit receives a virus from your home computer, it can deliver it to your hospital computer if you plug in your Fitbit at the hospital.

As I said before, whereas a criminal will merely shut down an active medical device or deny access to the machine, a terrorist won't ask for money; he will hack it to corrupt pharmacy records or to injure patients.

Auto-Hacking Attack

A lazy hacker will launch an **auto-hacking attack**. This is done with an easy-to-use device with an auto-hacking function that hacks into a hospital Wi-Fi network without a computer. The hacker goes into the hospital, simply turns on the device, selects a network, and the device hacks it automatically. It is a standalone machine and does not require boot from disc or computer. Hackers can also gain unauthorized access to the data on a target Bluetooth-enabled smartphone using a **Bluesnarfing attack** that uses wireless technology without alerting the user. Once inside a hospital network, a hacker will install at least one **backdoor.**

Backdoors

A *backdoor* is a means of access to a computer program that bypasses security mechanisms. Software programmers sometimes install a backdoor so that the program can be accessed for troubleshooting or other purposes. A backdoor also can be a hidden method for bypassing network authentication. The following are the two basic types of backdoors:

- **Beachhead backdoors**: Used to retrieve files, gather network and equipment information, and trigger execution of other capabilities.

- **Standard backdoors**: Communicates using HTTP protocol to blend in with legitimate web traffic or a custom protocol, and allows a hacker to upload/download, modify/delete/execute programs, modify the registry, capture keystrokes, harvest passwords and take screenshots.

Ad Hoc Network

Once inside the hospital network, a hacker can create an unauthorized **ad hoc network** (a wireless network that dynamically connects wireless client devices to each other without the use of an infrastructure device, such as an access point or a base station) to access a network that is not connected to the Internet. Unbeknownst to the hospital staff, some devices, such as network printers, contain built-in wireless capability that may not be used, so the default password remains unchanged. This is a huge vulnerability, because the wireless printer can be used as a wireless hub that relays hacker commands.

Unpatched Vulnerabilities

When a hacker discovers an **unpatched vulnerability** in the hospital network, he will use that to gain access. As I said before, less than 10 percent of network owners download software patches when they are announced. And, of course, a hacker will then load a virus onto a medical device because medical devices generally have almost zero security capability, not even authentication.

Appliance Hacks

A hacker can gain access to a hospital network through **appliance hacks.** With the growth of the Internet of Things, even common appliances such as dishwashers, coffee makers, clothes dryers, and nursery-room baby monitors connect to the Internet and could be used as an access and pivot point. Manufacturers use this capability to troubleshoot performance of their equipment, monitor usage, and improve the customer "experience." Unfortunately, knowing when you use the appliance provides data that could help hackers learn your habits and schedule, and geolocate your current position.

Password Cracker

Hackers have access to a wide range of tools to decrypt passwords that they find on a hospital network. The last resort is a **brute-force attack** using a program such as Zip Password Cracker Pro. This is a method of accessing an obstructed device through attempting multiple combinations of numeric and/or alphanumeric passwords. An attacker tries to use all possible combinations of letters, numbers, and symbols to enter a correct password. Any password can be cracked using the brute-force method, but it can take a very long time, so although this is very popular in movies, it is less so in real life. The longer and more intricate a password is, the longer it takes a computer to try all of the possible combinations. Table 2-4 offers password tips.

Table 2-4. *Cyber-Hygiene Password Tips*

Use strong password or passphrase.	Change password every 90 days.
Never use a previous password again.	Use lowercase and uppercase letters, numbers, and special characters ($, #, ?, %, &, etc.).
Do not use a common phrase (123thequickbrownfox, etc.).	Don't write down the password and slip it in the top drawer of your desk.
Password should be at least 14 characters.	Don't give anyone your password— ever.

If a hacker finds your hashed password file, he can use a custom tool to decode them and obtain the network administrator's password. A hacker can also use an **applet attack** to disable the Java security sandbox. Hackers then can gain access using an **ARP spoofing attack.** This is a technique by which an attacker sends (spoofed) ARP messages onto a hospital network. Generally, the aim is to associate the attacker's MAC address with the IP address of another host, such as the default gateway, causing any traffic meant for that IP address to be sent to the attacker instead. ARP spoofing may allow an attacker to intercept data frames on a network, modify the traffic, or stop all traffic. Often the attack is used as an opening for other attacks, such as denial-of-service, man-in-the-middle, or session hijacking attacks. It is also called *ARP cache poisoning* and *ARP poison routing*.

Denial-of-Service Attack

A denial-of-service (DOS) attack is when a hacker prevents or impairs the authorized use of networks, systems, or applications by exhausting network resources. A hacker can use a **teardrop DOS** that sends irregularly shaped network data packets to confuse the network servers. A hacker can use a **buffer overflow DOS** to flood a server with an overwhelming amount data.

A hacker can use a **Smurf DOS** that tricks other computers to reply to a fake request, causing much traffic. An **amplification attack** is another type of DOS that a hacker can use, in which a single UDP packet generates tens or hundreds of times the bandwidth to overwhelm a medical grade network with DNS response traffic.

Black Hole Attack

A black hole attack is a type of DOS attack in which a router that is supposed to relay packets instead discards them. This usually occurs from a router becoming compromised from a number of different causes. It is sometimes called a **packet drop attack**. One method mentioned in research is through a DOS attack on the router using a known DOS tool. Because packets are routinely dropped from a lossy network, the packet drop attack is very hard to detect and prevent. The malicious router can also accomplish this attack selectively; for example, by dropping packets for a particular network destination, at a certain time of the day, a packet every n packets or every t seconds, or a randomly selected portion of the packets. This is called a **gray hole attack**.

Generations of outbound network traffic pretending to be from somewhere else is a **spoofing attack**, typically used in a DOS attack. It is also called a **masquerading attack**.

Secondary Entry Points

A secondary access point is a device that allows another device to connect to a wired network. The following is an actual discussion between a SCADA security consultant and a potential client.

- Claim: "We are secure because the production network is completely separate from the rest of the corporate network." Client pulls out network diagram to prove his case.

- Flaw #1: But, the diagram doesn't match reality. It's the "desired" configuration, not the *actual* configuration. The network is accessible at several secondary access points.

- Flaw #2: Notebooks. Somebody plugged in a notebook computer when diagnosing an equipment failure and introduced a network worm (**Blaster**) that quickly spread.

- Flaw #3: SCADA network has zero protection. Once in production, the systems have never been patched and consoles have no authentication.

The skills of an "average" hacker are typically adequate to gain access once a secondary access point is identified. A hacker that is unable to get into a hospital network targets the hospital's suppliers. Vendors often list customers on their website s to impress potential clients and include detailed case studies of how customers implemented their systems and which products they installed. Cyber-security consultants have found the following information about their commercial customers through open source:

- Spreadsheets listing all accounts on network

- Maps of network, both physical and cyber

- Firewall policies

- Training materials for operators of the network

- Vendor manuals

- Source code for major applications

- Backup/sample configuration files for control systems

- Intranet search engine that made locating much of this easy

- Word, PowerPoint, Excel, and text files, including a listing of what the customer thought were things that hackers could do

Modems

Unbeknownst to a hospital, some vendors embed a modem in their equipment to allow remote vendor access via cell phone. This is an easy way to retrieve non-real-time data from a device. Most control devices have a model number, so it is a simple matter for a hacker to find the manual and compromise the device. Devices often have default passwords that were never changed since the device shipped, or contain backdoor usernames/passwords that can't be changed. Once an attacker hacks a device with a built-in modem, he owns that network node.

Rogue Access Points

A rogue access point is when someone installs a device without authorization that allows someone to connect to the network. Hospitals and healthcare facilities use hardwired and wireless networking to manage their assets. Even a hospital that does not use remote monitoring can have their networks compromised by insiders and rogue access points installed on their network. Utility company cyber-penetration tests tend to focus on Internet-connected systems and ignore the possibility of rogue access points operating wirelessly, so they are easily overlooked. A rogue access point installed on a BCS would allow an adversary to take down a hospital building from anywhere in the world. It is easy to overlook wireless rogue access points when you think a cyber-attack can only have an Internet vector.

CHAPTER 3

■ ■ ■

Active Medical Device Cyber-Attacks

Let me begin by saying I am not a doctor and I have zero medical training, but I do have over 15 years' experience in the Intelligence Community. Let there be no doubt in your mind, this book is about *the possibility of weaponization of medical devices by hackers* wishing to injure patients in healthcare facilities. This chapter describes *what I believe could happen* if an attacker is able to hack into a hospital network that controls the functions or parameters of a connected active medical device (AMD). An AMD is one that interfaces directly with a patient to administer medical treatment. I'm sure in some cases I may have missed the mark, but I assure you that a persistent terrorist will enlist the services of biomedical technicians to create a viable cyber-physical attack on a hospital's active medical devices if he so desires. The entire scope of armamentarium can be hacked.[1]

Many active medical devices today include a computer to control the machine and communicate with the network. The easiest way for a hacker to take control of an active medical device is to establish a connection with the device's computer and issue the appropriate commands directly. Most programmable logic controllers (PLC), protocol converters, or data acquisition servers lack even basic authentication and perform any properly formatted command received without question. Compared to regular corporate IT networks such as at a financial services or insurance company, a computer network at a healthcare institution is much more vulnerable.[2] Hospital IT defense in the United States is 10 years behind financial network defense and healthcare facilities are even more vulnerable because they typically do not have an IT staff with cybersecurity experience.

Researchers have found a number of examples of the compromise of medical devices including X-ray equipment, picture archive and communications systems (PACS) and blood gas analyzers (BGA). This includes diagnostic equipment (ultrasound, PET scanners, CT scanners, MRI, X-ray, etc.); physical therapy machines like continuous passive range of motion (CPM) machines; therapeutic equipment (infusion pumps, medical lasers and LASIK surgical machines); and life support equipment (heart-lung machines, medical ventilators, extracorporeal membrane oxygenation machines and dialysis machines).[3] Other equipment that can be hacked includes medical laboratory equipment such as those that analyze blood, urine, genes, dissolved gases in the blood and medical monitors such as ECG, EEG, and blood pressure machines. Even those new electronic stethoscopes can be hacked.

---

[1]Armamentarium means the equipment, methods, and pharmaceuticals used in medicine.
[2]TrapX Labs, "Anatomy of an Attack – MEDJACK (Medical Device Hijack)", May 7, 2015.
[3]Darleen Storm, "MEDJACK: Hackers Hijacking Medical Devices to Create Backdoors in Hospital Networks," *Computerworld*, June 8, 2015.

© Luis Ayala 2016
L. Ayala, *Cybersecurity for Hospitals and Healthcare Facilities*, DOI 10.1007/978-1-4842-2155-6_3

Researchers report that targeted hospitals are being attacked by an attack vector called MEDJACK (medical device hijack). According to a white paper by TrapX Labs, "MEDJACK has brought the perfect storm to major healthcare institutions globally," they warned. "Medical devices compromised by the MEDJACK attack vector may be the hospital's 'weakest link in the chain." According to TrapX, healthcare IT teams cannot access the internal software in medical devices, so they depend on manufacturers to build and maintain security in those devices. Yet manufacturers have not developed "the requisite software to detect most of the software payloads delivered by the MEDJACK attack."[4]

Attacking medical equipment is similar to hacking building equipment or industrial equipment, only the stakes are much higher because of the potential to harm patients. A hacker can attack the *operative system* of any machine (the part that actually performs the machine's intended function), or he can hack the *protective system* of a machine (the part that monitors the process for deviations from the expected results)— or he can attack both systems.

Generally speaking, when a "first failure" of the operative system occurs, the protective system detects the failure and transfers the device into a "safe state." So, for example, if a dialysis machine fails to operate properly, the protective system stops the blood pump, closes the venous clamp, and annunciates failure alarms. In such a machine, two independent failures are required before the machine operates in an unsafe condition. A single failure is probably not life threatening. Two independent failures would be life threatening—probably not a coincidence.

If the hacker is a *criminal* seeking to hold valuable medical equipment for ransom, he will attack the operative system, or the protective system, but not both. If the hacker is a *terrorist* seeking to cause injury to patients, he will attack both the operative system and the protective system. In the case of the dialysis machine, the terrorist hacker might shut down the heparin pump, change the mixture of the dialysate, disconnect the venous pressure monitor, and silence all alarms.

Finally, I want to point out that although vendors often tell customers they can't remove hard coded passwords from their devices or take other steps to secure their systems because it would require them to take the systems back to the U.S. Food and Drug Administration (FDA) for approval afterward. The truth is that FDA guidelines for medical devices include a cybersecurity clause that allows a post-market device to be patched without requiring recertification by the FDA.

Magnetic Resonance Imaging (MRI)

A common breach of MRI safety occurs when a metal object is attracted by the static magnetic field. Although generally considered very safe, if a hacker is able to tamper with the MRI controls, a person can be struck, injured, or trapped against the magnet by the object. The MRI may even be damaged by slamming into the magnet or struck by a rapidly accelerating object. These very high-strength magnetic field (or "missile-effect") accidents, where ferromagnetic objects are attracted to the center of the magnet have resulted in injury and death.[5] In one case, a six-year-old boy died during an MRI exam, when an oxygen tank was pulled across the room and crushed his head.[6]

A MRI device can displace implanted devices, heat devices through radiofrequency, or obscure the intended imaging. This is why all passive implants are labeled with specific information regarding their use within the magnetic resonance environment.

MRI requires a magnetic field that is uniform and strong. The field strength of the magnet is measured in teslas (T)—and while the majority of systems operate at 1.5T, commercial systems are available with a maximum magnetic field strength for clinical use of 19.8T. Each tissue returns to its equilibrium state after excitation by the independent processes of T1 (spin-lattice) and T2 (spin-spin) relaxation. To create

[4]Ibid.

[5]Randal C. Archibold, "Hospital Details Failures Leading to M.R.I. Fatality," *New York Times*, August 22, 2001.

[6]Valentina Hartwig, et al., "Biological Effects and Safety in Magnetic Resonance Imaging: A Review," *International Journal of Environmental Research and Public Health* (6), 2009.

a T1-weighted image magnetization is allowed to recover before measuring the MR signal by changing the repetition time (TR). To create a T2-weighted image magnetization is allowed to decay before measuring the MR signal by changing the echo time (TE). Tampering with the scanning parameters such as the repetition time or the echo time, number of slices, slice thickness, flip angle or Voxel size by a hacker would render the machine unreliable and possibly cause injury to the patient. Examples of potential MRI hacks are shown in Table 3-1.

Table 3-1. *Possible MRI Cyber-Physical Attacks*

Malicious Hacker Activity	Result
Spoof MRI to quench (drain) magnetic field	MRI ceases to operate when field collapses.
Override MRI strength of magnetic field	Potential tissue heating and burns for patient. Possibly damages the machine.
Cause machine to transmit more power than the coil was designed to manage	Can damage or ruin the machine or other electronics nearby.
Mute all alarms	Technician is unaware of hazardous conditions.
Turn off MRI, encrypt internal files	Interferes with MRI operation. A ransom is demanded to unlock MRI.
Change display information	Causes confusion as to the protocol.
Cause MRI to sound random alarms	Interferes with MRI operation.
Reboot the machine	Wipes out the configuration settings.
Cause the machine to associate one patient's file with another patient's image	Diagnosis delivered to the wrong patient.

X-ray Generator (X-ray)

Medical X-ray machines are used to take pictures of dense tissues. The radiation from X-ray machines are highly penetrating, ionizing radiation, therefore they can be very dangerous. X-rays are highly absorbed in soft tissue, and severe burns can result from exposure of the hands, arms, skin, or eyes to the primary or diffracted beams. The most common and earliest reversible change is the production of reddening of the skin or erythema. If the dose and energy is low enough reddening occurs, and then disappears; apparently, the effects are reversible with no future effects. Another reversible change is the loss of hair or epilation. It is possible to give a dose of radiation that will stop cell division in the epithelial cells so that hair ceases to grow temporarily and falls out. With a low dosage, the hair begins to grow after time, with no apparent permanent ill effects. A third reversible effect is when the sebaceous glands, which are temporarily affected, produce less sebum (oil secretion of these glands in the skin).

If a hacker is able to increase the dose or radiation exposure, a patient could be overexposed to enough radiation that it results in permanent destruction of either hair or sweat glands, or skin with a resulting scar. The irreversible changes are categorized as radiation dermatitis, chronic radiation dermatitis and radiation cancer. Acute exposure is a one-time event with high-level dose (>100 rem or 1 Sievert) and symptoms appear quickly (within days or weeks). Chronic exposures are long-term low-level doses and effects will appear slowly because the body has time to heal itself after exposure. The effects from chronic exposure, if any, appear 20 to 30 years after exposure.

A radiation burn can be an acute localized exposure that as a result of direct exposure to the primary beam. High-energy X-rays penetrate the outer layer of skin that contains most nerve endings, so the patient may not feel an X-ray burn until the damage has been done. Extreme cases require skin grafts or amputation of fingers. The severity of a burn depends on the dose received, the length of exposure, and the energy of the X-rays and the sensitivity of the patient. Burns can be caused with exposures at 300 rem, but normally are not apparent below exposures at 600 rem.

Radiation sickness can occur when a large dose is received to the whole-body. Symptoms will not appear unless the exposure is greater than 100 rem delivered within a few hours. Changes in blood tissue may be evident at low exposures. If a whole-body dose of 400 rem to 500 rem is received, approximately 50% of patients die within 30 days if untreated, and all suffer several months of illness. Acute exposure to a dose in excess of 700 rem to the entire body in a short period of time results in death within a few weeks.

Long-term effects of chronic exposure to ionizing radiation include carcinogenesis, life span shortening, and cataract formation with the principle delayed effect being an increased incidence of leukemia and other cancers. Examples of potential X-ray hacks are shown in Table 3-2.

Table 3-2. *Possible X-ray Generator Cyber-Physical Attacks*

Malicious Hacker Activity	Result
Increase voltage (kVp)	X-rays with higher keV photons.
Increase current (mA)	More X-ray photons (quantity).
Cause machine to exceed recommended radiation exposure for the procedure	Radiography (X-ray) extremity approximate effective dose is 0.001 mSv. Hacker can change the dose to 8 mSv (GI tract dose). Acute radiation exposure has potential for patient tissue heating, burns, or radiation sickness. High-level doses involved (>100 rem or 1 Sv). Radiation burns occur as a result of an acute localized exposure to the primary beam. High-energy X-rays readily penetrate the outer layer of skin that contains most of the nerve endings, so patient may not feel an X-ray burn until the damage has been done.
Mute all alarms	Radiologist is unaware of hazardous condition.
Turn off X-ray machine, encrypt internal files	Interferes with X-ray operation. A ransom is demanded to unlock the X-ray machine.
Change display information	Causes confusion about the radiation exposure received.
Cause X-ray to sound random alarms	Interferes with X-ray operation.
Cause the machine to reboot	Wipes out the configuration settings.
Cause the machine to associate one patient's file with another patient's image	Diagnosis delivered to the wrong patient.

Infusion Pump

Let me begin by saying that when used according to manufacturer instructions, infusion pumps are extremely safe to use and have an excellent track record. Manufacturers of infusion pumps are constantly improving the safety of their equipment and the next generation of "smart pumps" shows significant promise. An infusion pump delivers high-risk medications and critical fluids, medication, or nutrients into a patient's circulatory system; so if a hacker tampers with the delivery of fluids, it can have dire consequences. Like any other electro-mechanical device, safety features such as alarms and operator alerts can be defeated by a knowledgeable hacker.

The range of infusion pump safety features varies widely with the age and model of the pump. A state-of-the-art infusion pump would have these safety features:

- Have no single point of failure that would cause the pump to silently fail to operate properly. The pump warns the nurse with an audible alarm.

- The pump is equipped with batteries in case of a power interruption.

- Designed with anti-free-flow devices to prevent blood from draining from the patient, and prevent fluid from freely entering the patient during pump set up.

- A "down pressure" sensor that detects when the vein is blocked or the line is kinked.

- An "air-in-line" detector to detect when air is being pumped.

- An "up pressure" sensor that detects when the bag or syringe is empty.

- A drug library with customizable programmable limits for individual drugs to help prevent medication errors.

- Mechanism to avoid uncontrolled flow of drugs.

- An internal history log of the last several thousand therapy events.

Infusion pumps have been a source of multiple patient safety concerns, and problems with such pumps have been linked to more than 56,000 adverse event reports from 2005 to 2009, including at least 500 deaths. There were 87 recalls during this time and 70 were designated Class II (a category that implies medically reversible adverse health consequences or probable serious health consequences is remote). There were 14 Class I recalls (serious health consequences or death). The FDA has proposed stricter regulation of infusion pumps and launched an Infusion Pump Improvement Initiative.[7]

Many of the adverse events involving infusion pumps have been associated with software defects. Software errors can lead to over- or under-infusion. Other recalls addressed user interface issues, mechanical or electrical failures. The potential for over- or under-administration of critical fluids, drugs, food nutrients if a hacker gains control of an infusion pump can be life threatening. If an infusion is equipped with a central wireless capability, a hacker may be able to change the occlusion level, purge rate, bolus rate, dosage profile (flow rate, delivery volume, delivery time) and KVO (keep vein open). A hacker can even change the user interface screen to display what was originally entered by the medical practitioner while delivering a different and possibly harmful dose.

In short, infusion pumps can be a source of injury if hackers are able to send malicious commands directly to the device. Examples of potential infusion pump hacks are shown in Table 3-3.

---

[7]Food and Drug Administration Infusion Pump Improvement Initiative, http://www.fda.gov/MedicalDevices/ ProductsandMedicalProcedures/GeneralHospitalDevicesandSupplies/InfusionPumps/ucm202501.htm

Table 3-3. *Possible Infusion Pump Cyber-Physical Attacks*

Malicious Hacker Activity	Result
Spoof pump with low battery message	Pump ceases to communicate with hospital network.
Override patient pendant button	Pump does not administer pain medication when requested, or provides too much when patient pendant button is pushed.
Spoof pump that door is open	Pump pauses administering medication. Observation should be used to ensure quantity matches—visual verification is needed.
Spoof pump that total dosage was delivered when only partial was done	Patient does not receive full dosage prescribed.
Cause pump to misidentify barcode and download wrong parameters from the drug library for drug being administered	Incorrect autoprogram is administered with incorrect bolus; loading dose, constant fixed-rate, and lockout limit, causes over- or under-infusion, and possibly exceed dose upper limit.
Defeat purge process, alter purge rate	Air may not be removed from the syringe line.
Spoof occlusion pressure	Pump pauses administering medication.
Mute all alarms	Nurse is unaware when pump fails.
Turn off pump, encrypt internal files	Patient does not receive medication. A ransom is demanded to unlock pump files.
Change stored protocols in pump memory	Patient receives incorrect therapy, possibly exceeding dose limit.
Cause pump to prime continuously	Patient does not receive medication.
Change display information	Causes confusion as to what drug was given, what loading dose, and so forth.
Cause pump to sound random alarms	Interferes with patient therapy.
Cause the pump to reboot	Wipes out the configuration settings.

Positron Emission Tomography (PET) Scanner

A PET scanner is a nuclear medicine, functional imaging technique that is used to observe patient metabolic processes. The system detects pairs of gamma rays emitted indirectly by a positron-emitting radionuclide (tracer), which is introduced into the body. Three-dimensional images of tracer concentration within the body are then constructed by computer analysis. PET scanning involves exposure to ionizing radiation. The standard radiotracer used for PET has an effective radiation dose of 14 mSv. For comparison, radiation dosage for other medical procedures range from 0.02 mSv for a chest X-ray and 6.5–8 mSv for a CT scan of the chest. For PET-CT scanning, the radiation exposure can be 23–26 mSv (for a 150-lb. person). Examples of potential PET scanner hacks are shown in Table 3-4.

Table 3-4. *Possible PET Scanner Cyber-Physical Attacks*

Malicious Hacker Activity	Result
Mute all alarms	Nurse is unaware when PET fails.
Turn off PET, encrypt internal files	Diagnostic images held hostage. Hacker demands a ransom to unlock PET files.
Change stored protocols in PET memory	Incorrect diagnostic protocol followed.
Cause PET to sound random alarms	Interferes with patient diagnostics.
Cause the machine to reboot	Wipes out the configuration settings.
Cause the machine to associate one patient's file with another patient's image	Diagnosis delivered to the wrong patient.

X-ray Computed Tomography (CT) Scanner

A CT scanner is also called *X-ray computed tomography* (X-ray CT) or computerized axial tomography scan (CAT scan), and it uses X-ray images taken from different angles to produce cross-sectional (tomographic) images (virtual 'slices') of specific areas of a scanned patient, allowing the physician to see inside the patient without cutting. CT is regarded as a moderate- to high-radiation diagnostic technique; however, the radiation doses received from CT scans are 100 to 1,000 times higher than conventional X-rays.

A typical plain film X-ray involves radiation dose of 0.01 to 0.15 mGy, while a typical CT can involve 10–20 mGy (milligray) for specific organs, and can go up to 80 mGy for certain specialized CT scans. The effect of radiation is cumulative, and the more a patient is exposed, the greater the cancer risk. Long-term effects of chronic exposure to ionizing radiation include an increased incidence of leukemia and other cancers. Examples of potential CT scanner hacks are shown in Table 3-5.

Table 3-5. Possible CT Scanner Cyber-Physical Attacks

Malicious Hacker Activity	Result
Increase voltage (kVp)	X-rays with higher keV photons.
Increase current (mA)	More X-ray photons (quantity).
Alter configuration files and change radiation exposure limits that set the amount of radiation patients receive	Radiography (X-ray) extremity approximate effective dose is 0.001 mSv. Hacker can change the dose to 8 mSv (GI Tract dose). Acute radiation exposure has potential for patient tissue heating, burns, or radiation sickness. High-level doses involved (>100 rem or 1 Sv). Radiation burns occur as a result of an acute localized exposure to the primary beam. High-energy X-rays readily penetrate the outer layer of skin that contains most of the nerve endings, so patient may not feel an X-ray burn until the damage has been done.
Mute all alarms	Radiologist is unaware of hazardous condition.
Turn off CT machine, encrypt internal files	Interferes with CT operation. Hacker demands a ransom to unlock X-ray machine image files.
Change display information	Causes confusion as to the radiation exposure received.
Cause CT to sound random alarms	Interferes with CT operation.
Change threshold value of radiodensity that was set by the operator	Operator cannot separate different structures, making segmentation impossible.
Cause the machine to reboot	Wipes out the configuration settings.
Cause the machine to associate one patient's file with another patient's image	Diagnosis delivered to the wrong patient.

Defibrillators

A malicious hacker may be able to corrupt a Bluetooth-enabled defibrillator to deliver random shocks to a patient's heart or prevent a shock from occurring.[8]

Medical Ventilator

A medical ventilator is a machine designed to mechanically move breathable air into and out of the patient's lungs. Ventilators may be equipped with monitoring and alarm systems for patient-related parameters (e.g., pressure, volume, and flow) and ventilator function (e.g., air leakage, power failure, and mechanical failure), backup batteries, oxygen tanks, and remote control.

Modern ventilators are electronically controlled by a small embedded system to allow exact setting of pressure and flow characteristics to an individual patient's needs.

A mechanical ventilation system is classed as a life-critical system because a failure may result in death, so precautions are taken to ensure that mechanical ventilation systems are highly reliable (including the power supply). Hacking a mechanical ventilator is less likely compared to other pieces of equipment because they have simple safety valves, which open in the absence of power to act as an anti-suffocation valve that alarms if its mechanisms or software fail. Ventilators are generally not networked and don't allow web administration, so someone would have to have physical access to the devices to alter them. Examples of potential ventilator hacks are shown in Table 3-6.

---

[8]Kim Zetter, "It's Insanely Easy to Hack Hospital Equipment," *Wired* Magazine, April 25, 2014.

Table 3-6. *Possible Ventilator Cyber-Physical Attacks*

Malicious Hacker Activity	Result
Spoof pressure, volume, or flow alarm	Nurse cannot find source of problem. Interferes with patient procedure.
Alter patient-related parameters (e.g., pressure, volume, and flow)	Interferes with patient procedure with possibly serious adverse consequences.
Mute all alarms	Nurse is unaware of hazardous condition.
Cause the machine to reboot	Wipes out the configuration settings.

Anesthetic Machine

An anesthetic machine is used for the administration of anesthesia. The most common type of anesthetic machine is the continuous-flow anesthetic machine, which is designed to provide an accurate and continuous supply of medical gases (such as oxygen and nitrous oxide), mixed with an accurate concentration of anesthetic vapor (such as isoflurane), and deliver this to the patient at a safe pressure and flow. Modern machines incorporate a ventilator, suction unit, and patient monitoring devices. Anesthesia equipment are *generally not networked* and don't allow web administration, so someone would have to have physical access to the devices to alter them. Examples of potential anesthetic machine hacks are shown in Table 3-7.

Table 3-7. *Possible Anesthetic Machine Cyber-Physical Attacks*

Malicious Hacker Activity	Result
Spoof oxygen failure alarm	Ritchie whistle sounds when oxygen pressure is 38 psi (pounds per square inch) descending. Newer machines have an electronic sensor.
Disable Nitrous cut-off or oxygen failure protection device	The nitrous-oxide regulator is a "slave" of the oxygen regulator (i.e., if oxygen pressure is lost then the other gases cannot flow past their regulators).
Disable hypoxic-mixture alarms	Hypoxy guards (ratio controllers) prevent gas mixtures that contain less than 21% to 25% oxygen being delivered to the patient.
Mute all alarms	Anesthetist is unaware of hazardous condition.
Disable interlocks between the vaporizers	Designed to prevent inadvertent administration of more than one volatile agent concurrently.
Change display information	Makes it impossible to monitor the gases and cause confusion as to the flow for oxygen, air and nitrous oxide.
Cause machine to sound random alarms	Interferes with patient procedure.
Interfere with system monitoring the patient's heart rate, ECG, blood pressure, and oxygen saturation	Makes it impossible to monitor the inhaled and exhaled concentration or partial pressure of CO^2 (carbon dioxide), and an indirect monitor of the CO^2 partial pressure in the arterial blood.
Change the dosage doled out to patients	Possible catastrophic consequences (patient not fully anesthetized, overdose medication, drug-drug interactions).
Cause the machine to reboot	Wipes out the configuration settings.

Heart-Lung Machine

A heart-lung machine is used to provide blood circulation and oxygenation while the patient's heart is stopped. It is also referred to as an extracorporeal circuit (ECC) and is used to conduct cardiopulmonary bypass. Blood is drained by gravity to the heart-lung machine where it passes through an artificial lung (or membrane "oxygenator") and then is pumped back into the systemic arterial system. Heparinization is used to establish a safe level of anticoagulation. A heat exchanger is included in the oxygenator to offset the cooling of blood passing through the ECC as well as the frequent need to intentionally cool and then rewarm the patient. Examples of potential heart-lung machine hacks are shown in Table 3-8.

Table 3-8. *Possible Heart Lung Machine Cyber-Physical Attacks*

Malicious Hacker Activity	Result
Shut down heparin pump	Patient blood clotting possible.
Pump delivers too much heparin	High level of anticoagulation that must then be appropriately reversed. Blood may not clot correctly, causing internal bleeding, which if severe enough, can result in death.
Mute all alarms	Biomedical technician is unaware of hazardous condition.
Change display information	Confuses biomedical technician.
Cause machine to sound random alarms	Interferes with patient procedure.
Cause the machine to reboot	Wipes out the configuration settings.

Extracorporeal Membrane Oxygenation (ECMO)

ECMO is an extracorporeal technique of providing both cardiac and respiratory support to persons whose heart and lungs are unable to provide an adequate amount of gas exchange. Examples of potential ECMO hacks are similar to the heart-lung machine hacks shown in Table 3-8.

Dialysis Machine

A dialysis machine is designed to replace many of the kidney's important functions and restore a patient's blood to a normal, healthy balance by filtering out harmful wastes, salt, and excess fluid. A doctor creates a vascular access into the patient's blood vessels so the patient can be connected to the filtering machine during each hemodialysis session. The blood flows at a preset rate through a special filter inside the machine. The filter removes wastes and extra fluids from the blood, but retains the proper balance of minerals such as potassium and sodium. Once the blood is cleaned, it is then returned to the patient. When operated properly, dialysis machines are very safe and reliable. Although there are a very small number of reported deaths from technical failure in the presence of dialysis machines, the number of fatal accidents related to human error is high.

A dialysis machine is a diverse machine with an "operative system" (the part that actually performs the machine's intended function; for example, the dialysis proportioning system), and the "protective system" (the part that monitors the process for hazardous deviations; for example, temperature compensated conductivity monitoring). The dialysis machine is designed so when a failure of the operative system occurs, the protective system detects the failure and transfers the dialysis machine into a "safe state." So, if a dialysis machine fails, the protective system annunciates failure alarms, stops the blood pump, and closes the venous clamp.

In a dialysis machine, two independent failures are required before the machine operates in an unsafe condition. A single failure is probably not life threatening. Two independent failures, however, would be life threatening—not a coincidence. Examples of potential dialysis machine hacks are shown in Table 3-9.

Table 3-9. *Possible Dialysis Machine Cyber-Physical Attacks*

Malicious Hacker Activity	Result
Spoof extracorporeal venous pressure decrease	Biomedical technician assumes disconnect of needle from patient vascular access.
Spoof mechanical hemolysis alarm	Biomedical technician assumes obstruction in the extracorporeal circuit.
Shut down heparin pump	Patient blood clotting possible.
Disconnect the venous pressure monitor	Shuts down the pump.
Spoof machine air sensor	Air detector alarm causes pump to shut down.
Display message: T1 – Test Failed	Biomedical technician assumes machine is defective.
Mute all alarms	Biomedical technician is unaware of hazardous condition.
Change dialysate mixture proportions	Acute poisoning with a dialyzable substance.
Change display information	Confuses biomedical technician.
Spoof false patient high blood pressure alarm	Biomedical technician shuts down pump.
Cause machine to sound random alarms	Interferes with patient procedure.
Cause the machine to reboot	Wipes out the configuration settings.

Medical Lasers

Medical lasers are medical devices that use precisely focused light sources to treat or remove tissues (such as tumor removal, cataract removal, breast surgery, cosmetic dermatology, plastic surgery, prostatectomy and other surgical procedures). Medical lasers are also used to correct nearsightedness, farsightedness, and astigmatism, as well as photodynamic therapy. As with any type of surgery, laser surgery has potential risks. Risks of laser surgery include incomplete treatment of the problem, pain, infection, bleeding, scarring, and skin color changes. There are many different types of lasers, but only about a dozen laser systems are found in everyday clinical use. Different medical lasers are designed for a wide range of treatments and each has risks when not being used as designed. Beam hazards describe the direct effect of the laser energy on the skin or eye. Non-beam exposure concerns include compressed gases, cryogenic material, and carcinogenic materials.

Most treatment lasers used in surgery are Class IV because they are designed to deliver laser radiation for the purpose of altering biological tissue. Misuse of an infrared (IR) laser that is thermal in nature may result in permanently damaged tissue. Laser surgical procedures requiring high irradiance levels are also more likely to produce laser-generated airborne contaminants (LGAC) which have been shown to have mutagenic and carcinogenic potential.

Different laser wavelengths affect various parts of the human eye and may cause serious injury at high power levels. Laser radiation in the near-infrared region of the spectrum (700nm to 1400nm)[9] is invisible to the human eye and is very dangerous. Since the eye does not have an aversion response in the near- or far-infrared portion of the spectrum we do not know that a patient has been overexposed until the injury occurs.

---

[9]nm=nanometer

Injury severity from a laser depends upon the following parameters: wavelength, energy, aperture size, divergence, continuous or pulsed emission, the absorption characteristics of the tissue exposed, and the circumstances surrounding the exposure (duration and distance). Examples of potential medical laser hacks are shown in Table 3-10.

Table 3-10. *Possible Medical Laser Cyber-Physical Attacks*

Malicious Hacker Activity	Result
Change display information	Deliberately confuses medical laser technician.
Cause the machine to reboot	Wipes out the configuration settings.
Cause machine to sound random alarms	Interferes with patient procedure.
Mute all alarms	Medical laser technician is unaware of hazardous condition.
Tamper with the correction factors used in the determination of exposure durations	Threshold limit value (TLV)[10] for laser energy could exceed limits resulting in patient experiencing adverse effects.
Alter the number of pulses in an expected exposure situation (pulse repetition frequency)	Irradiance could exceed the TLV for continuous-wave exposure above the maximum permissible exposure.
Take laser out of standby mode	Laser becomes very hot; possible loss of coolant.
Put laser in standby mode	Interferes with patient procedure.
Sound leakage alarm	Surgeon stops the procedure.
Increase or decrease actual power	Laser output becomes unstable, possibly causing pitting in the lens.
Spoof display energy and actual energy	Actual energy different from display energy.
Display nitrogen error message	Surgeon stops the procedure.

Robotic Surgical Machine

A robotic surgical machine is used to aid in many types of surgical procedures, including urology, cardiology, colon and rectal surgery, gynecology, neurosurgery, and vascular and transplant surgery. Robotically assisted surgery is a relatively new technology and is touted as minimally invasive with reduced bleeding and shorter hospital stays. Instead of directly manipulating the surgical instruments, the surgeon uses a live video feed and a computer to control the robotic arms and the end-effectors. The surgeon does not have to be present in the surgical suite, but can be anywhere in the world, leading to the possibility of remote surgery.

A recent longitudinal study released by the University of Illinois shows that while generally considered effective, reliability of the equipment (as is true with any new technology) has been spotty at best.[11] The study shows that over a 14-year period, 8,061 malfunctions have been reported in the United States, resulting in 1,391 injuries and 144 deaths. The types of malfunctions reported included uncontrolled movements and spontaneous powering on/off of the machine, which caused 52 injuries and one death; loss of quality video feeds and/or reports of system error codes, which caused 41 injuries and one death; electrical sparks causing unintended burning of body tissues linked to 193 injuries; and unintended operation of instruments.

---

[10]The threshold limit value (TLV) of a chemical substance is a level to which it is believed a worker can be exposed day after day for a working lifetime without adverse health effects.

[11]H. Alemzadeh, et al., "Adverse Events in Robotic Surgery: A Retrospective Study of 14 Years of FDA Data," http://www.ncbi.nlm.nih.gov/pubmed/27097160.

The study also shows the procedure was interrupted requiring restart of the system 3.1% of the time. Surgeons had to convert to non-robotic procedures 7.3% of the time, and had to reschedule the procedure 2.5% of the time. The study shows an average of 550 adverse surgical events per 100,000 procedures. The study was prepared with information reported to the FDA MAUDE database from January 2000 to December 2013. There is the question as to whether the actual number of adverse events is actually higher because the information is self-reported. A law should be passed requiring it to be mandatory for surgeons to report events to public health authorities.

Robot reliability and safety problems are not limited to surgical applications. According to the British Health and Safety Executive, there were 77 robot-related accidents in 2005.[12] The point here is that these machines are very complex and require that experienced surgeons receive additional training in their use. In the past, surgeons concentrated on the surgical procedure. Now they are also concerned about possible equipment failures. We may soon have to add cyber-attack to their list of concerns. If a hacker can take control of a robotic surgery machine, a patient's life could be in danger. Examples of potential robotic surgical machine hacks are shown in Table 3-11.

Table 3-11. *Possible Robotic Surgical Machine Cyber-Physical Attacks*

Malicious Hacker Activity	Result
Change display information	Confuses medical laser technician.
Spontaneous reboot	Wipes out the configuration settings. Delay extends the procedure increasing time patient under anesthetic.
Cause machine to sound random alarms	Interferes with patient procedure.
Mute all alarms	Surgeon is unaware of hazardous condition.
Turn off video feed	Surgeon stops the procedure and converts to non-robotic procedure.
Cause uncontrolled movement or arms	Surgeon stops the procedure and converts to non-robotic procedure.
Turn off robot	Surgeon stops the procedure and converts to non-robotic procedure.
Cause network to drop packets	Interferes with patient procedure.

Medical Device Data Systems (MDDS)

Medical device data systems are networked hardware or software products that transfer, store, convert formats, and display medical device data. They can be hacked. An MDDS does not modify the data or modify the display of the data, and it does not by itself control the functions or parameters of any other medical device. An MDDS does not include devices intended for "active" patient monitoring[13] so the FDA down-classified MDDS from Class III (high risk) to Class I (low risk) because the FDA believes these devices pose a low risk to the public.[14] The FDA does not enforce compliance with regulatory controls for a MDDS such as an in vitro device intended for assessing the risk of cardiovascular diseases[15] or for use in diabetes management.[16] Examples of potential MDDS hacks are shown in Table 3-12.

---

[12]"Trust me, I'm a robot," *The Economist*, June 2006.
[13]Per government regulation, the word *active* represents "any device that is intended to be relied upon in deciding to take immediate clinical action" (21 CFR 8637 at 8644).
[14]21 CFR 880.6310
[15]21 CFR 880.9(c)(4)
[16]21 CFR 880.9(c)(5)

Table 3-12. *Possible Medical Device Data Systems Attacks*

Malicious Hacker Activity	Result
Deny information transfer	System fails to supply test information. Test must be repeated.
Delete or alter data	Test must be repeated.
Alter displays	Information garbled or misread.
Cause network to drop packets	Interferes with patient procedure.
Report false information	Causes staff to make incorrect treatment decisions.
Not report medical event	Interferes with patient treatment.
Report false medical event	Causes staff to make incorrect treatment decisions.
Alter transplant recipient list	Denies patient organs necessary for survival.

Active Patient Monitoring Devices

Active patient monitoring devices are networked in-hospital patient monitoring devices that require a timely response (e.g., a monitor that is intended to detect life-threatening arrhythmias, such as ventricular fibrillation or a device used to actively monitor diabetes for time-sensitive intervention). These devices can be hacked. If an attacker can hack an active patient monitoring device that receives and/or displays information, alarms, or alerts from a monitoring device, he can interfere with an alert that requires immediate, possibly life-saving attention. A good example is a nurse telemetry station that receives and displays information from a bedside hospital monitor, such as in an intensive care unit. Examples of potential active patient monitoring device hacks are shown in Table 3-13.

Table 3-13. *Possible Active Patient Monitoring Device Attacks*

Malicious Hacker Activity	Result
Deny information transfer	System fails to supply information such as alerting staff to an emergency situation.
Mute alarms	System fails to supply information such as alerting staff to an emergency situation.
Alter displays	Information garbled or misread.
Cause network to drop packets	Interferes with patient monitoring.
Display incorrect patient vitals	Causes staff to make incorrect treatment decisions.
Not report medical event	Interferes with patient treatment.
Report false medical event	Causes staff to make incorrect treatment decisions.

Interoperable Medical Devices

Interoperable medical devices are designed to be interoperable with other types of networked medical devices and with various types of health information technology. They can be hacked. The foundation for such intercommunication is hardware and software that transfer, store, convert formats, and display medical device data or medical imaging data. Technological advances of interconnected medical devices have proven to be a boon for patient care, particularly in cases where device-specific information, such as unique device identifiers (UDIs) and patient-specific data, such as electrocardiogram (ECG) waveforms, contained within a medical device can be relayed to other devices or used to fill electronic health records to improve health care decisions. However, if these devices communicate wirelessly or over a hospital network, they are vulnerable to cyber-attack—especially if they are IP-based.

One example of what can go wrong with interoperable medical devices involved a software-related problem corresponding to an ultrasound system that is part of an integrated system for the planning and delivery of intensity modulated radiation therapy (IMRT). The system provides precise delivery of radiation to tumors or other targeted tissues while minimizing the delivery of radiation to vital health tissue. The device was recalled because "the product has a software problem in which previous patient measurement data gets associated with another patient's image."[17] Examples of potential active patient monitoring device hacks are shown in Table 3-14.

Table 3-14. *Possible Active Patient Monitoring Device Attacks*

Malicious Hacker Activity	Result
Deny information transfer	System fails to supply critical information.
Alter displays	Information garbled or misread.
Cause network to drop packets	Interferes with patient monitoring.
Report false information	Causes staff to misdiagnose patient condition and make incorrect treatment decisions.
Not report medical event	Interferes with patient treatment.
Report false medical event	Causes staff to misdiagnose patient condition and make incorrect treatment decisions.

Medical Image Storage Devices

Medical image storage devices provide electronic storage and retrieval functions for medical images. They can be hacked. The FDA does not enforce compliance with the regulatory controls, including registration and listing, premarket review, post market reporting, and quality system regulation for manufacturers of medical image storage devices.[18] Examples of potential medical image storing hacks are shown in Table 3-15.

---

[17]"Software-related medical device recalls raise security, privacy concerns," *InfoSecurity Magazine*, July 25, 2012.
[18]21 CFR 892.2010

Table 3-15. *Possible Medical Image Storing Attacks*

Malicious Hacker Activity	Result
Deny information transfer	System fails to supply critical information.
Corrupt test results	Information garbled or misread.
Cause network to drop packets	Interfere with patient monitoring.

Medical Image Communications Devices

Medical image communications devices provide electronic transfer of medical image data between medical devices over a computer network. They can be hacked. The FDA does not enforce compliance with the regulatory controls, including registration and listing, premarket review, post market reporting, and quality system regulation for manufacturers of medical image communications devices.[19]

One of the concerns here is embedded web services that allow devices to communicate with one another and feed digital data directly to patient medical records. When a team from Essentia Health was tasked to look for security problems by a large chain of Midwest healthcare facilities, a representative of Essentia Health found numerous vulnerabilities. "A lot of the web services allow unauthenticated or unencrypted communication between the devices, so we're able to alter the info that gets fed into the medical record ... so you would get misdiagnosis or get prescriptions wrong," he says. "The physician is taught to rely on the information in the medical records ... [but] we could alter the data that was feeding from these systems, due to the vulnerabilities we found."[20]

Medical Laboratory

An attacker that hacks a hospital's laboratory automation system (LAS) can shut down the fume hoods, refrigerators, biosafety cabinets, and other critical systems and devices. The hacker can also hold all the archived research data for ransom and crash all of the heating, ventilation, and air conditioning (HVAC) equipment. This is important because data from many laboratories is also transferred to CDC as part of national disease surveillance on a regular basis and used for notifiable disease conditions. They are reported on a weekly basis by state in the *Morbidity and Mortality Weekly Report*. Examples of potential medical laboratory hacks are shown in Table 3-16.

---

[19]21 CFR 892.2020
[20]Kim Zetter, "It's Insanely Easy to Hack Hospital Equipment," *Wired* Magazine, April 25, 2014.

Table 3-16. *Possible Medical Laboratory Attacks*

Malicious Hacker Activity	Result
Deny information transfer	System fails to supply critical information.
Alter lab equipment settings or test procedures	Corrupted test results.
Cause network to drop packets	Interferes with patient monitoring.
Corrupt laboratory test results	Causes doctor to misdiagnose patient condition and make incorrect treatment decisions, prescribe the wrong drugs or administer unwarranted care.
Alter work orders	Interferes with patient treatment.
Contaminate samples	Causes inappropriate treatment to be administered.
Lose patient samples	Interferes with patient treatment.

Electronic Health Records (EHR)

Hospitals rely heavily on a clinical data warehouse, translational bioinformatics, clinical informatics, health information systems, and patient records. A hacker can use a **diagnostic server attack** to execute the following attacks without any authentication required, while maintaining stealthiness:

- remote memory dump
- remote memory patch
- remote calls to functions
- remote task management

A hacker that can access electronic health records can alter the data to cause physicians to misdiagnose, prescribe the wrong drugs, administer unwarranted treatment of cause the patient to forego needed treatment. Without access to secure electronic health records, doctors would have to resort to old-fashioned communications techniques like telephones and fax machines.[21] Examples of potential EHR hacks are shown in Table 3-17.

---

[21]"Cyber attack snarls Los Angeles hospital's patient database," Reuters, Feb. 17, 2016.

Table 3-17. *Possible Electronic Health Records Attacks*

Malicious Hacker Activity	Result
Modify patient's electronic health record	Hacker can change information (blood type, diabetic, etc.). Modification of patient health record is a means to create a situation that could harm or kill a patient.
Delete data	Patient history is lost.
Alter patient treatment history	Interferes with treatment (prevent accurate diagnosis).
Cause network to drop packets	Interferes with patient procedure.
Alter medication history	Interferes with treatment procedure. A medicine given in the wrong dose or to the wrong patient might leave someone injured or dead.
Alter treatment work orders	Possible catastrophic consequences (amputate wrong leg, overdose medication, drug-drug Interactions).
Misinform clinician	Possible harm to patient.
Alter test or treatment schedule	Interferes with treatment procedure.
Alter the medical information of an organ donor	Invalidates the organs for use, invalidates a patient's candidacy, uses organs for wrong patient.

Barcode Scanning Systems

Though not really a "medical" device, hospitals and healthcare facilities rely heavily on the use of medicine and bloodwork barcode scanning devices to track patient name and identification information (i.e., the barcode values), patient care, prevent medical errors. A hacker can manipulate these devices to report correct scans of patient labels when there is in fact a mismatch. Pharmacists rely on barcode information in the medicine inventory system to ensure patient safety by checking multi-drug interactions including alcohol, food, supplements, and diseases.

By tampering with the barcode system, a hacker can manipulate the flow of blood samples or medications within the hospital, resulting in the delivery of the wrong medicine types and dosages, as well as mix up blood samples. Altering the data when a patient file, wrist band or medication label is scanned can result in life-threatening situations that would be difficult to unravel when time is of the essence.

A terrorist hacker may be able to corrupt sample-tracking software and cause barcode scanners to store scanned information in the wrong patient file. Drug-drug Interactions would likely occur with severe consequences. Finding these errors in massive patient files would be extremely difficult.[22] Physicians rely heavily on digital medical records that can be altered by a hacker to cause physicians to misdiagnose illness, prescribe the wrong drugs, or administer unwarranted care. Examples of potential barcode scanning system hacks are shown in Table 3-18.

---

[22]JA Ansari, "Drug Interaction and Pharmacist," *Journal of Young Pharmacists*, July–Sept. 2010.

Table 3-18. *Possible Barcode Scanning System Attacks*

Malicious Hacker Activity	Result
Alter patient scan information	Hacker can change information (blood type, diabetic, etc.).
Delete barcode data	Patient history is corrupted or lost.
Alter patient treatment history	Interferes with treatment (prevent accurate diagnosis).
Cause network to drop packets	Interferes with patient treatment.
Alter medication history	Possible misdiagnosis.
Alter treatment work orders	Possibly catastrophic consequences (amputate wrong leg, overdose medication, drug-drug Interactions).
Misinform clinician	Possible harm to patient.
Alter treatment schedule	Delays medical test or treatment.

CHAPTER 4

■ ■ ■

Medical Facility Cyber-Physical Attacks

Not only are active medical devices in the hospital building at risk of cyber-physical attack, the hospital building itself can be targeted. In the past, hospitals experienced nuisance cyber-attacks such as ransomware, website defacement, or theft of patient data. A cyber-physical attack on a hospital building has the potential to do serious physical damage to critical hospital equipment and interfere with patient care.

Attackers can hack something as simple as hospital refrigerators used to store blood and drugs by changing the temperature settings to cause spoilage. On the subject of hospital refrigeration systems for blood and pharmaceutical storage and cryogenics, a representative of Essentia Health says, "They all have a web interface that allow you to set the temperature range." **A hacker capable of altering climate controlled transport or storage of organs could corrupt the organs and deny a patient the life-saving treatment he needs.** Hospital refrigeration systems provide email alerts to notify hospital staff if the temperature falls outside acceptable ranges, but the systems are only protected by passwords. Once a hacker gains access to the system, he can turn off the notification feature or alter the settings for who and when an alert is sent.[1]

Building Controls System

A hospital's building controls system (BCS) monitors and operates the environmental equipment (boilers, air conditioning, cooling towers, carbon dioxide, carbon monoxide, temperature, relative humidity, noise levels, etc.) to maintain a comfortable and safe environment, as well as reduce energy and water consumption. The BCS can shut off water in the hospital, close outside air vents, and turn up the heat. If the emergency generators come on, a hacker with control of the BCS can cause them to damage themselves by simply making them think that they are overheating or by signaling that there is no fuel so the generators shut down automatically. Elevators can be made to go up and down continuously without opening the doors, or to only stop between floors and open and close the doors at random.

A BCS typically consists of thousands of network-controlled sensors and actuators, so the attack-surface is enormous. Whereas defenders have to block all the ways that hackers can get into the network, hackers only need to find one weak point. Many BCSs rely on programmable logic controllers, protocol converters, or data acquisition servers that lack even basic authentication and perform any properly formatted command without question. The easiest way for a hacker to take control of the hospital's building equipment is by establishing a connection with the equipment over the BCS and issuing the appropriate commands.

---

[1]Kim Zetter, "It's Insanely Easy to Hack Hospital Equipment," *Wired* Magazine, April 25, 2014.

© Luis Ayala 2016
L. Ayala, *Cybersecurity for Hospitals and Healthcare Facilities*, DOI 10.1007/978-1-4842-2155-6_4

Facility Equipment Controlled by the BCS

These are some of the systems and equipment typically controlled by a BCS:

- Backup electrical generators

- Transformers, auxiliary power units (APU), power distribution units (PDU)

- Switchgear (including load-shed controls)

- Lighting controls

- HVAC Air handling units (AHU) including variable air volume (VAV) boxes

- Ventilation systems and filters

- Fans, blowers, dampers

- Chillers, condenser water pumps

- Cooling towers

- Boilers and hot water heaters

- Chilled water system

- Potable water system

- All primary and secondary pumps and valves

- Sewage treatment system

- Occupancy sensors

- Alarms, public address system

- Fire sprinklers

- Uninterruptable power supply (UPS)

Unlike a corporate or enterprise network cyber-attack where data is stolen and an intrusion can go undetected for years, a BCS controls building equipment in real time so that a cyber-physical attack on facilities equipment is immediately discovered. Probing attacks mapping a BCS network can be conducted stealthily and go completely undetected. Causing a power outage and programming a large electrical backup generator to self-destruct does not go unnoticed.

Totally infallible cybersecurity is not possible, but choosing to stay out of the cyberspace domain by cutting all network ties with the outside world will significantly reduce the attack surface. In addition, although we may not be able to prevent viruses from infecting a hospital network or computer, we can reduce the possibility of damage to critical building equipment. Without water, power, and cooling, a hospital cannot operate effectively for very long. Increased reliance on the commercial power grid and **installation of networked sensors and controls at hospitals over the last 15 years has increased the vulnerability to cyber-exploitation and reduced equipment reliability**.

Can hospital facilities be made more resistant to cyber-attack? Hospital BCSs are more robust than most buildings. Hospitals can maintain high availability with backup generators and store potable water on site; however, these elements must be protected from cyber-physical attack. What follows is a description of the various types of building equipment failures that could impact hospital operations.

Depending on the type of hospital or healthcare facility being attacked, the biggest targets of a cyber-physical attack are the building utilities (electricity, water, gas, sewer), and HVAC systems. Other targets are secondary in that they are less likely to result in catastrophic failure and generally are not life-safety considerations. A hacker will attack a single point of failure first. He attacks equipment or systems that cause other systems to fail. For example, shut off the water to the building and the mission will continue, albeit somewhat degraded; however, shut off the electricity and everything shuts down—eventually. If the hacker can damage the building switchgear or transformers, it won't matter if the uninterruptable power supply works or the backup generator fires up. Electricity will not be distributed properly through the building. What's worse is that large transformers today are manufactured overseas, so replacement of damaged or destroyed equipment could take months. I recommend your hospital contract with a local construction company for priority on-call maintenance support. When a hacker damages critical building equipment, you will want a general contractor on site immediately.

BCS Network Vulnerabilities

Several factors contribute to the increased risk to hospital BCS networks:

- Standardized BCS software has well-known vulnerabilities.

- Connectivity of hospital BCS network with other hospital networks is common.

- Technical information about BCS equipment and controls is publicly available.

- Default weak or blank passwords.

- Passwords used by former hospital employees are often still active.

- Unauthorized or undocumented equipment on the hospital BCS network.

- Unpatched BCS security software.

- A successful cyber-physical attack on a BCS network would deny, degrade, or disrupt hospital operations and could cause permanent damage to sensitive building equipment that cannot be replaced quickly.

- Most BCS devices do not support encryption, so a determined hacker could sniff network communications and collect information on hospital operations.

- A hacker who controls the hospital BCS network could deny authorized users access to the network to restore critical services. A hacker could send false messages and alter any sensor data transmitted over the BCS network.

- A hacker can use the BCS to cause equipment to appear as if working properly when in fact it is not, so maintenance personnel would remain unaware and delay response to an emergency.

- Changing operating thresholds on devices could make them shut down at lower values or fail to shut down automatically at higher values.

Due to their critical nature, life safety equipment manufacturers typically use proprietary electronic controls, and although more difficult to access, these too can be disrupted.

Although software does not wear out, corrupt software is what makes digital instrumentation and a BCS vulnerable to cyber-physical attacks. Software does not fail in the same sense that mechanical components fail. A cyber-attack manipulates software to force equipment to work incorrectly (i.e., it does not perform its intended function), perform erratically, or simply cease to function.

Cyber-physical attacks need not be overly complex. A simple cyber-attack can be initiated by sending a confusing signal that an intelligent electronic device does not recognize as a valid command. Generally, the device shuts down until a valid command is received. A mischievous hacker could cause nuisance equipment failures or failures designed to confuse maintenance personnel into thinking breakdowns are mechanical in nature, when in reality, the equipment is functional (it performs as it is being instructed).

A common cause failure (CCF) is a slow process caused by corrosion or premature wear of mechanical components. A second-order CCF, such as motors and pumps that to cease to function when commercial power is lost, is easily fixed by restoring electricity. This is not the case for equipment that relies on software to operate and control critical building operations.

When a full-scale cyber-attack shuts down the commercial power grid, hospital backup generators will probably also be targeted for cyber-physical attack. An enemy bent on attacking the United States will see to it that the outage causes physical damage to critical (long-lead) equipment so that commercial power could not be restored for weeks or months. It may take six months to replace one backup generator.

My book *Cyber-Physical Attack Recovery Procedures* (Apress, 2016) explains in greater detail how to determine if a cyber-physical attack on a building is underway and how to mitigate the event, so I won't go into that here. Suffice it to say, when a hacker attacks your hospital or healthcare facility, there are things that you should do and there are things that you shouldn't do. It is possible sometimes to predict a cyber-attack if you know what the precursors to a cyber-attack look like and actively watch for them. It is also possible to slow down a cyber-attack and prevent the hacker from doing any more damage. There is also a protocol to be followed for law enforcement purposes and a requirement for a proper chain of custody for evidence.

Preventing Hospital Building Equipment Damage

Traditional IT-focused security solutions are unsuitable for equipment control networks such as a BCS. A BCS uses computers to monitor performance of equipment, sensors, and devices, and it adjusts device parameters to accommodate changes due to weather or building occupancy. Even under normal network traffic, broadcast messages can overload some building equipment controls and cause them to crash. Making a hospital cyber-secure may be easier than securing IT-focused networks, because although you cannot stop all viruses from infecting a computer, you can stop an infected computer from damaging hospital building equipment and medical devices.

Various equipment vendors have developed network security "appliances" that create zones of security as recommended by ISA/IEC-62443 standards.[2] For example, the Xenon Security Appliance manufactured by Tofino, Inc., is installed into an existing network with no changes to the network, forming "conduits" of communications between zones. If a cyber-attack originates from a secondary entry point, the potential damage is contained within the zone in which the attack originated and does not spread across the entire network (see Figure 4-1).

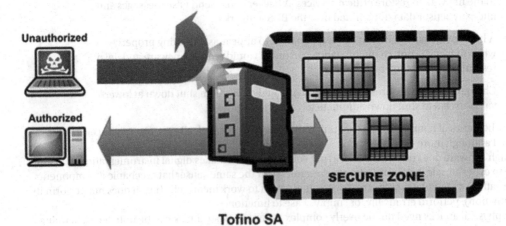

Tofino SA

Figure 4-1. Xenon Security Appliance manufactured by Tofino (I highly recommend.)

---

[2]ISA = industry standard architecture. IEC = International Electrochemical Commission.

The controls engineer defines rules that specify which network devices are allowed to communicate and what protocols they may use. Any network traffic that does not fit the rules is automatically blocked by the appliance and reported as a security alert. Deep packet inspection allows detailed filters to enforce security policy, such as only allowing read commands to be sent to a programmable logic controller.

Facility Equipment Cyber-Physical Attacks

The following is a partial list of cyber-attack hazards capable of being carried out via BCS systems to disrupt mission-essential functions (single or multiple cyber-attack vectors simultaneously).

- Denial-of-service, force continual equipment hardware reboots
- Shut off building utilities (electric, water, sewage pumps)
- Turn equipment off or continuously cycle rapidly
- Sever hospital communications
- Take security and alarm systems offline (CCTV, sensors)
- Change operating parameters (temperature, outside air ventilation levels)
- Set off false alarms
- Display phantom error messages
- Delete or overwrite data files
- Erase or corrupt system memory
- Conceal activity on the network
- Overspin motors and pumps
- Hide valid hospital equipment-failure notifications
- Change user passwords (privilege escalation)
- Lock out maintenance personnel from BCS access
- Contaminate potable water supply (backflow)
- Crash all systems simultaneously and change network configuration

My book on cyber-physical attack recovery procedures describes the types of things that a hacker can do to building equipment in detail, but I will briefly touch on the major items here.

Steam Boilers

A *boiler* is a closed pressure vessel in which water or other fluid (hydronic) is used to heat a building, while a *furnace* uses warm air. The heat is different, and the way that heat is circulated through the building is different. Once in your BCS, a hacker can send any one of many locking and blocking error codes to the boiler to shut it down. Interrupting the fuel that feeds the boiler or furnace or interfering with the combustion process is problematic, at best, but a boiler that has a loss of feed water and is permitted to boil dry can be extremely dangerous. If feed water is then sent into that empty boiler, the small cascade of incoming water instantly boils on contact with the superheated metal shell and leads to a violent explosion that cannot be controlled, even by steam safety valves.

Boiler Sequence Controller Hack

Boiler controller, burner programmer, burner controller, sequence controller, and programmable sequence controllers measure the temperature of the combined water flow of a multi-boiler installation. They are pre-programmed for the automatic operation of gas/oil burners and regulate the number of boilers in operation to match the required demand. They continuously monitor the flame and can control how many boilers fire up at one time for safe startup. They provide output for blower, ignition, and solenoid valves with prefixed timing for continuous flame supervision. Hack this and all the boilers can be turned on full blast.

Hot Water Heater Explosion

Fire departments are familiar with the explosive potential of a hot-water heater. If a hacker can cause the hot-water heater tank (a pressure vessel) to flash into explosive failure at 332°F, the explosion will hurl burning debris in all directions with tremendous force. Equipment several rooms from the point of the explosion become airborne and people in the mechanical room can be injured or killed as the water heater explodes. It is important to remember that the blast from an explosion in a mechanical room will travel through building ductwork. I have seen air vents on the other side of a building blown out from a blast event.

Chillers

Chillers are not as dangerous as steam boilers or pressure vessels, but a hacker can wreak havoc with your chillers if he knows what he's doing. The old absorption chillers generated hydrogen gas naturally as a result of the reaction of lithium bromide with the steel surfaces of chiller, but they are not very common anymore. A hacker attempting to disrupt the chilled water system will generally tamper with the refrigerant flow or the condenser water temperature. If a hacker can cause the pressure differential (lift) to exceed the capacity of the compressor, the backward pressure flow will cause the chiller to surge. Conversely, if the hacker can cause the pressure in the evaporator to drop, that can also cause the compressor to surge. If the compressor surges, you will know it because it is very noisy and it trips the breaker.

The cooling tower can also cause the compressor to surge with reduction in the flow of water to the condenser. If the cooling tower fan stops, you will get a high temperature condition. Of course, the hacker would have to defeat the low temperature safety switch, so it does not shut down the chiller automatically. Chiller surge will cause damage to the rotating assemblies. When a second or lag machine must be started, the timing of the isolation valves is crucial in preventing a surge condition. If the valve does not open after 90 seconds, the lag system automatically shuts back down in a failure mode.

If a hacker shuts down the chiller and leaves the pump on, the water in the system heats up, increasing the pressure on the cooling side of the chiller. That will increase the pressure in the chamber, causing the rupture disc to fail, releasing the refrigerant into the atmosphere. If the refrigerant is R-11, maintenance personnel can be overcome, and being unable to breathe, possibly pass out from lack of oxygen. This is not the case with R-34 refrigerant. Of course, repairing the rupture disc and replacing lost refrigerant will take time; you should be back up and running in a couple days (provided you have a preferred maintenance agreement with the building equipment vendor).

Cooling Tower

A *cooling tower* is used to dispose of unwanted heat from a chiller. Water-cooled chillers operating on the principle of evaporative cooling are normally more energy efficient than air-cooled chillers. To achieve better performance (more cooling), they are designed to increase the surface area and the time of contact between the air and water flow. A *collection basin* is used to collect and contain the cooled water after its interaction with the airflow. Makeup water is added to the system to compensate for water lost due to evaporation.

Cooling tower water is filtered to remove particulates and treated with biocides and algaecides to prevent growths that could interfere with the continuous flow of the water and prevent the growth of *Legionella* bacteria, including species that cause Legionnaires' disease, most notably *L. pneumophila*, or *Mycobacterium avium*. Cooling towers are fitted with electrical immersion heaters, steam coils, or hot water coils in the collection basin to prevent freezing. Obviously, the basin heater should not be operating in the summer because it would contribute to the growth of opportunistic pathogens.

Modern cooling towers are designed with a drift eliminator that provides multiple directional changes of airflow to prevent the escape of water droplets. They are designed to prevent excessively high water levels and possible overflow of the cold-water basin due to over pumping, clogged strainers, or makeup valve malfunction.

A hacker wishing to disrupt a building HVAC may decide to flood the cooling tower collection basin, turn off the fans, and heat the water in the basin. Turning off the pumps or intermittent fan reversal would also cause damage to the cooling tower, chillers, or both. Another hack is to search the installation files to determine the resonant operation speed of the unit, which may result in vibrations that could damage the components or structure, and/or create objectionable noise. The resonant speed ranges are identified at startup and are typically locked out to prevent the variable frequency drive to operate the motor at these resonant speeds. A hacker may also interfere with the chemical "pot" feeder that injects diluted liquid biocides directly to the collection water basin.

Another possible hack would be to spoof the vibration cutout switch (VCOS) to shut down the cooling tower. A VCOS is designed to cause a trip condition when it detects any vibration after a time delay. A VCOS can be mechanical or electronic with a single setpoint containing one trip limit for alarm or shut down.

Backup Generator

In 2007, CNN broadcast a demonstration of an Aurora cyber-physical attack of a 2.25-megawatt diesel generator connected to a substation that ended with an explosion that sent engine parts flying as far as 80 feet. This test was conducted at the Idaho National Laboratory (INL) for the US Department of Homeland Security (DHS). INL staff injected a virus consisting of 20 lines of code that caused an out-of-phase condition that can damage alternating current (AC) equipment connected to the power grid.

Connecting AC equipment out of phase is a known vulnerability, but doing it maliciously was brought to light by the test conducted by INL. This condition occurs when a circuit breaker or breakers are opened and closed rapidly, resulting in an out-of-phase condition. The test demonstrated the threat associated with rapidly disconnecting and reconnecting a generator to the grid, but out of phase—via physical or cyber intrusion of control systems conducted maliciously or unintentionally.

Because an Aurora event consists of the out-of-sync reconnecting of three-phase rotating equipment, just about any three-phase equipment (motors, generators) can be attacked. Risk mitigation is achieved by placing a hardware device that monitors for the rapid out-of-phase condition associated with an Aurora event between each substation and its loads. The device isolates the substation from its loads before the torque of the grid can be applied to the equipment. Cooper Power Systems and Schweitzer Engineering Laboratories are relay-protection suppliers that manufacture digital protection and control devices (DPCD) capable of closing breakers that can adversely impact critical electrical rotating equipment. These devices are relatively inexpensive and have wiring configurations similar to other relays.

A hacker can break into the BCS through an *enterprise network access point* (a device that logically connects wireless client devices operating in the building infrastructure and provides access to a distribution system, if connected, which is typically a hospital's enterprise wired network).

A hacker that can access your BCS can use *alarm flooding* (the annunciation of more alarms in a given period of time than a human operator can respond to) to confuse maintenance personnel. Ten alarms per minute are typically the most alarms that a technician can handle.

CHAPTER 5

■ ■ ■

Hospital Insider Threat

In 2011, Cybersecurity Watch Survey[1] revealed that 60 percent of cyber-attacks come from outside entities. Sad to say, according to an IBM report,[2] 55 percent of all attacks in 2014 were carried out by malicious insiders or were inadvertent mistakes. A malicious insider with access to a hospital network has the potential to do the most physical damage to medical equipment and hospital facilities. Insider threats to critical infrastructure are more serious than outsider threats because an outside attacker is less likely to know the hospital network vulnerabilities and its weaknesses as well as an insider would. The following are the primary insider threats:

- Employees (and contractors) not following security protocols.

- Employee logging into an unsecured network, accidentally releasing a worm into the corporate network.

- Sloppy password administration (vendor default passwords not changed, ex-employee passwords not deleted and accounts not deactivated, passwords not changed regularly).

- Incorrectly installed systems unintentionally bridge networks together.

- Improperly protected human-machine interface (HMI).

- Unauthorized hardware/software on the network (keylogger, wireless transmitter).

Insiders pose a cyber-threat because an employee could escalate access privileges in order to modify controls, turn equipment on/off, or drive equipment to failure. An insider can plant a worm or a Trojan horse in a hospital network that can be activated quickly to cause multiple failures without further intervention. The insider could then pretend to attempt to fix the problem, meanwhile stepping around the true causes. The insider threat includes vendors who provide maintenance and support (typically via network or dial-in modem connections).

Types of Insider Threats

There are several categories of insiders, which can be further divided into those jobs that require an employee to have access to the BCS network and those that do not (see Table 5-1).

---

[1]B. Brenner, "Report: Insider attacks expensive, but there's a silver lining," *CSO*, Feb. 3, 2011.
[2]*IBM 2015 Cyber Security Intelligence Index*. Last accessed May 11, 2016 at http://public.dhe.ibm.com/common/ssi/ecm/se/en/sew03073usen/SEW03073USEN.PDF

© Luis Ayala 2016
L. Ayala, *Cybersecurity for Hospitals and Healthcare Facilities*, DOI 10.1007/978-1-4842-2155-6_5

Table 5-1. *Insider Threat Types*

Insider Types	Descriptors
Insider (current or ex-employee)	Employee, contractor, vendor, utility company technician
Insider associate	Has limited authorized access and escalates privileges
Insider affiliate	Insider by virtue of an affiliation; spoofs the identity of the insider
Outsider affiliate	Non-trusted outsider that uses an access point that was left open

Why would a hospital employee want to damage the hospital building or medical equipment? According to the FBI, these are the major reasons:

- **Greed or financial need**: A belief that money can fix anything. Excessive debt or overwhelming expenses.

- **Anger/revenge**: Disgruntlement to the point of wanting to retaliate against the hospital.

- **Problems at work**: A lack of recognition, poor performance rating, disagreements with co-workers or hospital administration, dissatisfaction with the job, a pending layoff, or passed over for promotion.

- **Ideology/identification**: A desire to help the "underdog" or a particular cause.

- **Divided loyalty**: Allegiance to another person or to a country besides the United States.

- **Adventure/thrill**: Want to add excitement to their life, intrigued by the clandestine activity, a "James Bond wannabe."

- **Vulnerability to blackmail**: Extra-marital affairs, gambling, fraud.

What type of employee behavior would indicate that a hospital employee might be a threat? The behavioral characteristics of attackers are potential indicators and patterns to detect insider threat activity. Figure 5-1 shows many types of observable employee behavior to look for which could serve as precursors to malicious activity. No one behavior by itself would be an issue, but questionable behaviors are more likely to be manifested in multiple observables.

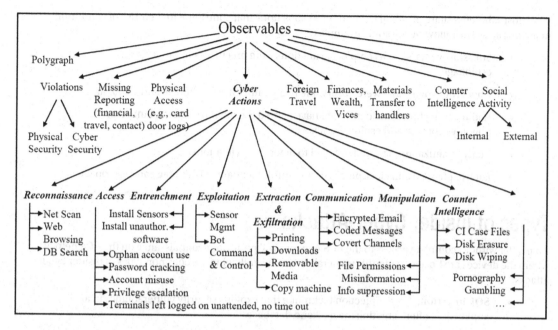

Figure 5-1. *Insider threat observable behaviors (Maybury 2006)[3]*

A great deal of research has been done concerning counterproductive work behavior in an effort to discover precursors by looking at personality predispositions. A study by Baron and Neuman[4] posits that organization changes (e.g., pay cuts, changes in management) frequently led to aggression. Robert Willison and Merrill Warkentin found perceived injustice as a common motivator for sabotage.[5] A study by FEMA's Community Emergency Response Team's (CERT) Management and Education of Risks of Insider Threat (MERIT) project comparing IT sabotage and espionage identified personal predispositions and stressors as precursors of malicious events.

Insiders historically telegraph their intent by exhibiting counterproductive work behavior. The following are some examples:

- Not following security protocols.

- Log in to an unsecured network and release a worm into the corporate network.

- Sloppy password administration.

- Incorrectly install systems that bridge disparate networks together.

- Improperly protected HMI.

---

[3]M. Maybury, "Detecting Malicious Insiders in Military Networks," in MILCOM-06 Washington, DC, 2006.

[4]J. Neuman and R. Baron, "Workplace violence and workplace aggression: Evidence concerning specific forms, potential causes, and preferred targets," *Journal of Management*, 1998.

[5]Robert Willison and Merrill Warkentin, "Beyond Deterrence: An Expanded View of Employee Computer Abuse," *MIS Quarterly*, Volume 37, Issue 1 (2013).

Most saboteurs share personal issues or predispositions that contribute to their risk of committing malicious acts. The following are some examples:

- Stressful events, such as employer sanctions were precursors of sabotage and espionage.

- Concerning behaviors were observable before and during sabotage and espionage.

- Actions by technical insiders could have alerted the organization to planned or ongoing sabotage and espionage acts.

- Many organizations ignored or failed to detect rule violations.

- Lack of physical and electronic access controls facilitated IT sabotage and espionage.

Types of Insider Cyber-Attacks

An insider without complete access to the BCS network will perform reconnaissance on the BCS network where the devices are hosted to identify vulnerabilities. The following are common types of insider cyber-attacks:

- **SQL injection**: A code injection technique that exploits security vulnerabilities in an application, often targeting the backend database.

- **Default credentials**: Attempt to log in to secure areas using default credentials.

- **Dictionary attack**: A brute-force attack against a human-machine interface. HMIs with no lockout mechanisms can allow attackers to attempt multiple logins with little effort and no repercussions.

- **Modbus traffic attack**: Attempt to modify and execute valid commands issued by the HMI to the PLC (Modbus protocol sends traffic in clear text without requiring authentication).

- **Denial or disruption of service**: A denial of service attack could include shutting down routers, closing access to ports, deleting files, and renaming a server so other machines do not recognize it.

- **Buffer overflow**: An overflow occurs when hacker sends more data than the buffer expects, and nearby data is overwritten.

- **Spoofing**: Spoofing exploits weaknesses in protocols to spoof users or reroute traffic. Spoofing servers allows hacker to gain unauthorized remote login, and flood the network with garbage packets to knock a computer, sensor, or control device off the network.

An insider can use Cain and Abel software, which is a powerful multipurpose tool that can then sniff and crack passwords. The insider can also load a virus, such as those shown in Table 5-2, on to a network.

Table 5-2. *Computer Virus Types*

Virus	Description
Boot virus	Infects the boot sector of floppies or hard disks
Macro virus	Written in Microsoft Office macro language
Network virus	Spreads via network shares
Stealth virus	Hides in a file, copies itself out to deliver payload
Polymorphic virus	Encrypts itself
Cavity virus	Hides in the empty areas of executables
Tunneling virus	Traces interceptor programs that monitor OS Kernel requests
Camouflage virus	Disguises themselves as legitimate files

It's important to note not all insider events are malicious; some, though well meaning, can be just as harmful. We know of an employee that downloaded a malicious worm that he thought was an antivirus program.

Next, we look at the type of hacking tools used by insiders.

Insider Hacking Tools

Software

There are many hacker software tools readily available by free download that can analyze weak and vulnerable machines in a network with just a few clicks. Primarily designed for use over the Internet, these tools can easily be used by an insider directly on the network.

Hardware

In addition to software (which is difficult to detect), an insider can install physical devices on the hospital network or on any workstation for unauthorized access to the hospital network. There are numerous hacker devices that can be used to compromise a hospital network. For example, KeyGhost and KeyPhantom are keylogger devices that can be installed on a PC to capture every keystroke entered on that machine. Devices can be programmed to transmit the data over the network to an insider's machine, or the information can be transmitted wirelessly to a confederate. These devices are difficult to detect and not easily discovered because they are made to look like they belong on the equipment.

CHAPTER 6

■ ■ ■

Detection of Cyber-Attacks

Detecting most incidents requires automated analysis tools, system behavior patterns, and an awareness of what to look for among equipment operators, supervisors, and other hospital staff. Hackers try to hide their activities by stealing large amounts of data during peak hours. They deliberately limit the amount of data they steal at any one-time and use common protocols like HTTP or SSL.[1] Hackers also choose a logical pivot point to attack that allows them to spread their malware across the hospital network. The attention of medical equipment operators and the building maintenance engineers is critical to detection of unusual operations and they are usually the first to notice anomalies in equipment and system behavior.

Indicators of a Possible Cyber-Attack

Here is a quick list of signs to look for from the US-CERT Intruder Detection Checklist that indicate your system may have been compromised:

- Examine log files for connections from unusual locations or other unusual activity
- Look for setuid and setgid files (especially setuid root files)
- Check system binaries to make sure that they haven't been altered
- Check systems for unauthorized use of a network monitoring program
- Examine files run by "cron" and "at"
- Check for unauthorized services
- Examine /etc/passwd file and check for modifications to that file
- Check system configuration and network configuration for unauthorized entries
- Look everywhere for unusual or hidden files

There are many indicators that indicate a cyber-incident has taken place. Any one indicator by itself is not enough to raise an anomaly from the level of *cyber-event* to *cyber-incident*. However, if you see a number of these indicators at the same time, that is a cause for concern. Table 6-1 is a list of indicators of a cyber-physical attack.

---

[1]HTTP=Hypertext Transfer Protocol and SSL is Secure Sockets Layer

© Luis Ayala 2016
L. Ayala, *Cybersecurity for Hospitals and Healthcare Facilities*, DOI 10.1007/978-1-4842-2155-6_6

Table 6-1. *Cyber-Attack Indicators*

Unusually heavy network traffic

Out of disk space or significantly reduced free disk space

Unusually high CPU usage

Creation of new user accounts

Attempted or actual use of administrator-level accounts

Locked-out accounts

Accounts in use when the user is not at work

Cleared log files

Full log files with an unusually large number of events

Antivirus or IDS alerts

Disabled antivirus software and other security controls

Unexpected patch changes

Machines or field devices connecting to outside IP address

Requests for information about the system (social engineering)

Unexpected changes in configuration settings

Unexpected system shutdown

Stoppage or displayed error messages on a web, database, or application server

Unusually slow access to hosts on the network

Filenames containing unusual characters or new or unexpected files and directories

Auditing configuration changes logged on the host records, especially disabling of auditing functionality

A large number of bounced emails with suspicious content

Unusual deviation from typical network traffic flows

Erratic equipment behavior, especially when more than one device exhibits the same behavior

Any apparent override of safety, backup, or failover systems

Equipment, servers, or network traffic that has bursts of temporary high usage when the operational process itself is steady and predictable

Unknown or unusual traffic from corporate or other network external to control systems network

Unknown or unexpected firmware pulls or pushes

Cyber-Attack Detection Tools

Wireshark is a network protocol analyzer that lets you see detailed information about what's happening on a network. Kismet and NetStumbler are wireless network detectors. They passively collect packets and can detect rogue access points and hidden networks. Snort is a network intrusion detection system that can detect probes or attacks and stealth port scans. A stealth port scan is designed to probe a server or host for open ports without being detected. The purpose is to identify services running on a host and exploit vulnerabilities.

Intrusion Detection Systems

An intrusion detection system (IDS) is a device or software that monitors for possible security breaches, which include both intrusions (attacks from outside the organization) and misuse (attacks or malfeasance from within organizations) and reports incidences. An IDS alerts us whenever it detects suspicious behavior, such as any of these events:

- Unauthorized user logging in

- Virus or Trojan horse detected

- Rapid and/or continuous logins/logouts

- Users logging in to accounts outside of normal working hours

- Numerous failed login attempts

- User accounts attempting to escalate account privileges

- Suspicious software and/or configurations on a server or workstation

- Unusual system behavior)

- Irregular process found

- Spontaneous reboots or screen saver change

- Unusually slow performance or usually active CPU

- CPU cycles up and cycles down for no apparent reason

- Intermittent loss of mouse or keyboard

- Configuration files changed without user or system administrator action in operating system

- Configuration changes to software made without user or system administrator action

- BCS unresponsive

- When an asset is communicating outside the bounds of the data flow baseline

- HMI, OPC, and controllers not synchronized

- Unexpected changes to instructions, function calls, commands, or alarm thresholds being sent from HMI[2] or OPC[3] to controllers

- HMI or OPC not updating after operator made changes to instructions, commands, or alarm thresholds

- Expected changes to controllers are not appearing on controllers

- An irregular vendor patch coming from an external source, or unexpected source, to a device within the BCS

- A device on the BCS is communicating with an undocumented, unauthorized, or unknown IP address

---

[2]HMI is the Human Machine Interface, typically a computer monitor.
[3]OPC is the interoperability standard for the secure and reliable exchange of data in the industrial automation space and in other industries.

- A device other than authorized devices is sending field controller traffic to a BCS device

- Traffic coming or going to an unknown device)

- A BCS field controller is communicating with an unknown device

- A BCS device has expanded its communications to other devices within the BCS

There are two types of IDS:

- **Host-based intrusion detection** (HIDS) operates on information collected from within an individual computer. This vantage point allows host-based IDSs to determine exactly which processes and user accounts are involved in a particular attack on the Operating System. Furthermore, unlike network-based IDSs, host-based IDSs can more readily "see" the intended outcome of an attempted attack, because they can directly access and monitor the data files and system processes usually targeted by attacks.

- **Network-based intrusion detection** (NIDS) detects attacks by capturing and analyzing network packets at specific points that interface to the external environment and the network segment to be protected. Listening on a network segment or switch, one network-based IDS can monitor the network traffic affecting multiple hosts that are connected to the network segment. The NIDS looks for rule violations and reports incidences.

An example of a NIDS hardware device is the Xenon Security Appliance by Torfino Security. Any network traffic that does not fit the preset rules is *automatically blocked* by the appliance and reported as a security alert.

An active NIDS reacts by terminating services or blocking hostile behavior. The active NIDS prevents damage by a quick response and are best used with knowledge-based detection (this is more likely to slow down system performance). A passive NIDS also sends alerts or sounds an alarm. A passive NIDS is easier to deploy, but slows down response time.

There are many "observables" in the real world and the virtual world that tell that us something is going on that we need to explore. Most alerts are not malicious and are due to authorized events or can otherwise be explained. You should first ask the following questions:

- Was maintenance performed on the system or a software update installed recently?

- Did the equipment simply malfunction?

- Did the equipment lose network connectivity (outside the building)?

- Was a new BCS device installed?

- Was a BCS device reconfigured? Was it reconfigured correctly?

- Were other authorized events causing excessive network traffic?

- Was an old process removed from the BCS?

- Could it have been user error?

If an event is detected *and* it cannot be explained, then we are compelled to perform *integrity checks* on *every* server, workstation, router, network switch, firewall, controller, all printers, and peripherals. *When* an event is detected that may be a cyber-attack, an event ticket is created and the appropriate Incident Response Team is called upon to investigate.

Air-gap computers, firewalls, demilitarized zone (DMZ), network nodes, multifactor authentication, and encrypted communications prevent script kiddies[4] from attacking hospital equipment. Those defenses may also discourage criminals from trying to get in because it's easier to try the doorknob next door than invest time and energy in trying to defeat a well-defended network.

Although not always the case, past cyber-attacks have been analyzed and certain "precursors" have been detected, but many are easily ignored. The first indication that a cyber-physical attack is underway might be BCS alarms sounding that a piece of building equipment has failed. A sophisticated attack will use several zero-day[5] vulnerabilities so antivirus solutions looking for known malware signatures won't detect it. Automated detection via applications or routines, such as network monitors, network traffic analysis applications, IDS and antivirus programs that can detect and flag malware, intrusion attempts, policy violations, and exploits may help determine the actual presence of hackers, but equipment failure and operator observation of abnormal system or equipment) behavior will likely appear first.

Intrusion Detection System Alarms

Because of the complexity of BCS installations, every alarm that pops up does not necessarily mean the BCS is under attack. It is rare to see a BCS status screen in a security operations center (SOC) where the alarm notifier is *not* blinking red. Most SOCs have a full screen of faults detected in the systems that need attention. Some of the alerts are caused by coms failures, or sensors and controllers that failed or need to be reset. Alarms tend to fall into one of four categories:

- **True Positive:** Something bad happened and the IDS caught it.

- **True Negative:** The event is benign and no alert was generated.

- **False Positive:** The IDS alert sounded, but the event was not malicious.

- **False Negative:** Something bad happened, but the IDS did not catch it.

The method of detection used by the IDS affects the number of false positives generated. Behavior-based (anomaly) detection can detect previously unknown attacks, but is prone to false positives. On the other hand, knowledge-based (signature) IDS only detect known attack profiles.

Intrusion Prevention System

An intrusion prevention system (IPS) is a device that can detect intrusive activity and attempt to stop the activity before it reaches its target. Automated prevention is not recommended below the control systems field point of connection because the preventive action could result in unintended consequences.

---

[4]A *script kiddie* is an unskilled individual (typically juvenile) who uses scripts or programs developed by others to attack computer systems and networks and deface websites. Their objective is to try to impress their friends or gain credit in computer-enthusiast communities.

[5]A *zero-day exploit attack* is a worm, virus, or other cyber-threat that hits users on the same day that the vulnerability is announced.

Firewalls

A firewall is a hardware/software capability that limits access between networks and/or systems in accordance with a specific security policy.[6] There are four types of firewalls:

- **Packet filters**: Twenty-year-old technology, inexpensive, least secure, compares each packet against a list of rules.

- **Circuit-level gateways**: More secure than packet, inexpensive, operates at layer 4.

- **Application-level gateways**: Application-specific, moderately expensive. Operates at layer 5.

- **Stateful, multi-layer inspection firewall**: Highest cost, most effective. Provides layer 3 filtering, layer 4 validation, and layer 5 inspection.

Firewalls are low-cost solutions and have been used successfully when they have been "hardened" by doing the following:

- Turning off all but essential services/daemons and protocols required

- Limiting user accounts, require strong authentication to access the system

- Not sharing authentication services with trusted hosts on the network

- Configuring to only open essential ports

- Configuring for full logging with high integrity (read-only encrypted local logs or logged to a remote system or a read-only device)

- Shutting down as many utilities and configuration tools as possible

- Keeping the system fully patched

- Removing all unnecessary applications, and

- Running an IDS on the system

Antivirus Programs

It's always a good idea to use antivirus software for individual workstations and home computers. Each antivirus program has its advantages and disadvantages, so you need to decide which is best for your use. I prefer an antivirus solution that uses "whitelisting". A whitelist is a list of programs that are allowed to execute. Whitelisting is the reverse of "blacklisting", the practice of identifying programs that are denied, unrecognized, or ostracized.

Three examples of very good antivirus programs that I recommend are listed below (in no particular order):

- Avast Pro Antivirus 2016

- Webroot SecureAnywhere

- Bitdefender Antivirus Plus 2016

Whitelisting antivirus software provides protection in real-time by blocking malware execution. Good antivirus software prevents the user from visiting malware-hosting websites (blacklisting) or downloading malware to a computer. Some antivirus software is designed to roll back everything the program did after detecting malicious activity. Keep in mind that some events can't be rolled back.

---

[6]"Secure Data Transfer Guidance for Industrial Control and SCADA Systems," Pacific Northwest National Labs, PNNL-20776, Sept. 2011.

Webroot SecureAnywhere anti-virus software is designed to prevent man-in-the-middle attacks, browser process modification and keylogging. Webroot is effective at preventing ransomware from encrypting files. Webroot leaves the good files alone, eliminates the bad programs and monitors unknown programs. If an unknown program tries to exfiltrate your data while it's being monitored, it won't succeed.

Bitdefender is an excellent product as well, however ransomware protection is turned OFF by default and must be ENABLED.

Forensic Evidence of a Cyber-Attack

The following are strategies suggested by AusCERT, a not-for-profit organization based at The University of Queensland, Australia, that relies on member subscriptions to cover operating costs.

Rootkits

A rootkit is software much like a Trojan horse that hackers use to perform a number of tasks, including the following:

- Capture information, such as user passwords.

- Install backdoors that can be accessed remotely.

- Hide its existence and therefore the fact that the system has been compromised.

- Allow the affected computer to be used as a pivot point for further exploitation.

The following products are used in rootkit detection:

- **rkdetect** available at `www.security.nnov.ru/soft/`

- **VICE** available at `www.rootkit.com`

- **BartPE** available at `www.nu2.ne/pebuilder/`

The following are things that you should look for:

- Examine log files for **connections from unusual locations** or for other unusual activity. This is not foolproof because many hackers edit or remove log files in an attempt to hide their activity.

- Look for **odd user accounts** and groups.

- Look for **unexpected user or group membership.** Some of the built-in groups give special privileges to the members of those groups. For example, members of the Administrators group can do anything to the local system. Backup operators can read any file on the system. Power users can create shares.

- Look for **unauthorized user rights**. To examine user rights, use the User Manager tool under Policies ä User Rights. There are 28 different rights that can be assigned to users or groups. Generally, the default configuration for these rights is secure.

- Look for **unauthorized applications starting automatically**. There are a number of different methods an intruder could use to start a back door program, so be sure to:

- Check the startup folders for **suspicious applications** (there are two startup folders: one for the local user and one for all users). Examine all the shortcuts. When a user logs on, all of the applications in both the All Users folder and in the local user startup folder are started.

- Check the registry.

- Look for **unauthorized services** and make certain they are necessary. Some backdoor programs are a Trojan horse or backdoor program that start when the system boots up.

- Check legacy files such as Autoexec.bat, Autoexec.nt, config.sys, system.ini, and win.ini for unauthorized changes.

- Check system binaries for **alterations**. Compare with copies you know that have not been altered. Be cautious of trusting backups; they could also contain malicious software (malware).

- Just checking file properties and timestamps is not sufficient for determining whether or not the programs have been replaced.

- Check network configurations for **unauthorized entries**. Look for invalid entries for settings such as WINS, DNS, IP forwarding, etc.

- Look for **unauthorized shares**.

- Check any **future jobs scheduled to run**. Hackers leave back doors in files that are scheduled to run at a future time. This technique can let a hacker back on the system (even after you addressed the original compromise). Verify that all programs referenced by the scheduler and the job files themselves, are not world-writable.

- Look for **unauthorized processes**. Use the Task Manager tool to gather information about the processes running on your system.

- Look throughout the system for **unusual or hidden files**.

- Look for **altered permissions** on files or registry keys. Secure the Windows system to limit permissions on files and registry keys so that hackers cannot start unauthorized programs or change system files.

- Look for **changes in user or computer policies**. Policies define a wide variety of configurations and can be used to control what users can and cannot do. Policies are configured via the local computer policy.

- Make sure that the **system has not been joined to a different domain**. A hacker may attempt to gain domain administrator access by changing the current domain to a domain that the hacker controls.

- Audit for **intrusion detection**.

Run Intrusion Detection System

The following are very good commercial intrusion detection tools:

- **Tripwire** available at www.tripwire.com

- **Real Secure Server Sensor** available at www.iss.net/products_services/enterprise_protection/rsserver/protector_server.php

- **eEye SecureIIS** available at www.eeye.com/html/products/secureiis/

- **Intact** available at http://pedestalsoftware.com/products/

CHAPTER 7

■ ■ ■

Preventing Cyber-Attacks

The first step in preventing a cyber-attack is to make sure that staff members are educated about potential threats, many of which arrive in their inbox. Hospitals are encouraged to enforce preventive behaviors that will benefit their entire network. Basic cyber-hygiene training of the workforce is a necessity. Good cybersecurity practices will not only save hospitals from paying a ransom, but also lawsuits. Target, for example paid $10 million to settle a class action lawsuit.

Cyber-Hygiene

According to the Canadian Cyber Incident Response Centre, fully *85 percent of targeted cyber-attacks are preventable*. Perfect cybersecurity is unachievable, and probably unaffordable, however, there are steps that can be taken to minimize the risk of cyber-attack against healthcare facilities.

Step 1. Physical Access to Equipment and Workplace

- Make sure that the MGN is not connected to the Internet or the enterprise network. Commercial organizations have been alarmed to discover through searches on Shodan that their network is indeed accessible over the Internet, despite assurances to the contrary. Such a discovery counteracts the folk-myth of "security by obscurity."

- Implement stringent physical access controls.

- Provide lockable or locking enclosures or rooms for system components (e.g., servers, clients, and networking hardware) and for the systems used to manage and control physical access (e.g., servers, lock controllers, and alarm control panels).

- Provide a method for tamper detection on lockable or locking enclosures.

- Change locks, locking codes, keycards, and any other keyed entrances when construction or renovation of the hospital is complete.

- Reprogram codes (e.g., remove default codes) on locks and locking devices so that the codes/passwords are unique to each hospital wing and do not repeat codes used in the past.

- Install MGN cabling that is routed thru unprotected areas in metal conduit.

- Provide two-factor authentication for physical access control.

© Luis Ayala 2016
L. Ayala, *Cybersecurity for Hospitals and Healthcare Facilities*, DOI 10.1007/978-1-4842-2155-6_7

- Have the equipment supplier verify and provide documentation that communication channels are as direct as possible (e.g., communication paths between devices in one network security zone do not pass through devices maintained at a low security level or cross unnecessarily into low security zones).

- Remove or disable all services and ports not required for normal operation, emergency operations, or troubleshooting. This includes communication ports and physical input/output ports (e.g., USB docking ports, CD/DVD drives, video ports, and serial ports). Document disabled ports, connectors, and interfaces.

- Install uninterruptable power supply for all computer equipment.

- Set the BIOS to only boot from the C drive.

Step 2. Eliminate Common MGN Vulnerabilities

- Key automation and control devices should be grouped into zones that share common security-level requirements.

- Do not permit remote access to the MGN from outside the building by anyone (maintain the air gap), including equipment vendors.

- Do not connect laptop computers to the MGN unless absolutely necessary. If you do, make sure that the laptop gets a thorough cleaning and is scanned for malware and spyware.

- Do not permit wireless control of devices inside mechanical rooms. Whenever possible, use point-to-point direct wired connections.

- Cyber assets and their communication media should be protected with a six-wall border to limit physical tampering with the systems and media.

- Install end-point protections on the servers, control consoles and all IP-enabled devices to prevent Stuxnet-like intrusion from insiders purposefully or haplessly installing malware from USB drives (or from installing external attack code that made it onto the MGN network).

- End points (CD-ROM, USB, RJ-45, RS-232, RS-485, LON connectors, terminal block connections, serial and parallel ports, jacks, plugs, etc.) should be monitored for security state, attempted access violations, malicious behavior and vulnerabilities. Most computer keyboards and mice plug into a USB port and a common *USB thumb drive can be made to emulate a keyboard or a mouse* to defeat a weak USB defense, so the keyboard and mouse connectors should be glued in place.

- Detection devices should be used to identify any attempt to set up rogue communication devices, new systems, connectivity, applications, and wireless access. Maintain a list of approved MGN devices and the connectivity and communication profiles between devices.

- Disable unused ports as well as remote protocols that are insecure like Telnet.

- Disable all protocols that communicate inbound to your trusted resources, but are not critical to functionality.

- Require user name/password combinations for all systems, including those that are not deemed "trustworthy."

- Set appropriately secure login credentials. Do not use defaults.

- Implement two-factor authentication on all trusted systems for any user account.

- The most common configuration problem is credentials management (i.e., weak passwords, shared user accounts and insufficiently protected credentials), followed by weak or non-existent firewall rules and network design weaknesses.

- Change passwords frequently, and sometimes with no notice.

- Utilize network segmentation to secure resources like VES systems,[1] ICS, and medical devices.

- Make sure that trusted resources have the latest patches and that new patches/fixes are implemented when they are released. Implement a mandatory patch-management protocol.

- Use real-time anti-malware protection and real-time network scanning locally on trusted hosts and where applicable.

- Control access to trusted devices. For example, for access to a segmented network, use a bastion host with access control lists (ACLs) for ingress/egress access.

- Develop a threat modeling system for your hospital. Understand who is attacking you and why.

- The system health of each cyber asset should be monitored for suspected system use of memory, CPU, and number of network connections.

- Perform unscheduled, no-notice exercises to test network vulnerability to cyber-attack.

- Network activity logs should be encrypted.

- Use application layer encryption, and encrypt files stored on hosts and servers.

Step 3. Monitor Access to the MGN

- The system administrator should monitor all activity on the MGN network on a 24-hour basis. Keep and review network activity logs.

- Inventory all direct and indirect trusts and associations (e.g., personnel, vendors, contractors, supply chain partners). This can be done by monitoring access (including physical access, when relevant) over time. Pay particular attention to those with too much privilege such as administrators, who should not have super access to the entire system contents or use shared passwords.

- Improve logging in on trusted environments in addition to passing logs to SIEM devices[2] for third-party backup/analysis.

- Enforce strict controls and separation of duties (SoD) for direct access and monitoring of control room operators, administrators, and others with direct access.

- Monitor systems and networks users are accessing over time for typical behavioral information between these trusts, their applications, and their traffic.

---

[1]VES=virtual execution system
[2]SIEM= security information event management devices

- Assess and inventory all access to networks, systems, and specific resources.

- External personnel monitoring can be accomplished through content analysis of social media (e.g., LinkedIn, Facebook, Twitter, YouTube) using tools such as Maltego, content scraping, and search engines like Devon Technologies.

- Critical vendor partners should also be monitored for new business relationships, financial results, organizational changes, and governmental associations.

- Maintain workforce situational awareness and be on the lookout for counterproductive work behavior. Defined as intentional behaviors that are contrary to legitimate organizational interests, including sabotage and espionage. Watch for personal predispositions and stressors such as serious divorce, personal financial problems, mental health disorders, personality problems, social skills and decision-making biases, and a history of rule conflicts as precursors of malicious events.

- Avoid over-dependence on any insider (two-man rule).

- Address counterproductive work behavior consistently and fairly. A perceived variation in justice is a potential stressor. Researchers have found *perceived injustice as the most common cause of sabotage.*

- Monitoring insider behavior is particularly important when organization changes occur such as changes in management, organizational sanctions, or negative workplace events (e.g., pay cut, missed promotion, below-average performance appraisal).

- Question anomalous behavior (why is insider working outside of normal working hours?).

- Do not ignore security-policy rule violations. Enforce limits on access and hold individuals accountable for their actions.

- Watch for an insider *tipping point* (the first observed event at which an insider became disgruntled such as insider demoted, reprimanded for harassing coworker, or is being fired). Researchers have found that insiders *typically commit malicious acts within seven days of tipping point.* Look for drastic changes in behavior.

- Review the audit logs for actions or accesses that seem inappropriate. Reviews should be more frequent and extensive for individuals with higher privileges.

- Use intrusion detection methods to look for attack signatures or anomalies that indicate a network attack may be in progress or may have already occurred.

- Use network vulnerability scanners to assess the configuration of the MGN network, identify security deficiencies, and recommend countermeasures.

- Apply a digital signature to individual or combinations of event logs with sequence numbers to ensure that the event logs are complete.

- Use sophisticated tools to automatically scan large amounts of data to analyze event logs and to present suspicious events to the auditor in a user-friendly manner.

- Use intrusion detection tools to monitor transactions at the network layer based on the source and destination addresses and protocol types and can look for "signatures" of known attack scenarios and anomalous behavioral patterns.

- Remove any user accounts that are not needed for normal or maintenance operations.

- Do not permit user credentials to be transmitted or shared in clear text. Do not store user credentials in clear text.

- Institute a method for protecting against unauthorized privilege escalation.

- Have the supplier disclose the existence of all known methods for bypassing computer authentication (backdoors) and provide written documentation that all such backdoors have been permanently deleted from the system.

- Do not allow multiple concurrent logins using the same authentication credentials, do not allow applications to retain login information between sessions, do not provide any auto-fill functionality during login, and *never* allow anonymous logins.

- Restrict communication traffic between different network security zones.

- Install a host-based malware detection capability that will quarantine (instead of automatically deleting) suspected infected files. Update malware signatures and test and confirm compatibility of malware detection application patches and upgrades.

- *Ensure that passwords do not revert to default* after software patches are installed.

- Install antivirus software on all servers, point servers, and stations and adopt an active virus scanning strategy.

- Ensure that antivirus software does not exclude any directories from being scanned.

- Prohibit email clients or instant messaging on any node of the MGN.

- Use encryption whenever possible or use matched sets of equipment.

- Verify identity of outside visitors the day before arrival by contacting their home organization. Do not wait until the day of the visit to an East Coast facility if their home office is on the West Coast. If they come in the morning, they will be long gone by the time the office on the West Coast is open.

- Have a clear policy as to who should be contacted in the event of suspect activity.

Network Procurement Documentation

Before purchase and installation of network hardware and software can commence, the hospital IT personnel should insert the necessary language in the procurement documents to ensure that the designer understands the cybersecurity requirements. A good guide to follow is the DHS's *Cyber Security Procurement Language for Control Systems*. Key recommendations developed by the National Cyber Security Division are summarized in Table 7-1.

Table 7-1. *System Hardening Protection*

System Hardening Precaution	Rationale
1	Remove unnecessary services and programs.	Unused services and programs are possible entry points for exploits and are generally not monitored. Only services used for control systems operation and maintenance shall be enabled.
2	Provide host intrusion detection system.	It is difficult to detect unauthorized changes or additions to the operating system or application programs.
3	File system and operating system permissions	The operating system is shipped with default configurations that allow unneeded access to files, and loose configuration parameters that can be exploited.
4	Hardware configuration	Disable all unneeded communication ports and removable media drives, or provide engineered barriers. Password-protect the BIOS from unauthorized changes.
5	Heartbeat signals	Heartbeat signals or protocols can be corrupted, spoofed, or possibly used as an entry point for unauthorized access. Provide packet definitions of the heartbeat signals.
6	Install patches and software updates properly.	Systems ship with a number of well-known vulnerabilities and patches have been known to introduce security vulnerabilities or reverse security features (services, ports, permissions, revert back to default passwords, etc.) affected by the patch.
7	Firewalls	Vendor shall provide firewalls and firewall rule sets between network zones. This information is sensitive and shall be protected.
8	Disable, remove, or modify well-known or guest accounts	Default accounts and passwords are used on many control systems and are often publicly available in published materials.
9	Session management	Use access protocols that encrypt or securely transmit user-login credentials. Do not permit concurrent session logins, remembered account information between login, auto-filling of fields during logins, and anonymous services such as FTP.
10	Password/authentication policy and management	Vendor shall provide a configurable account password management system that allows for selection of password length, frequency of change, complexity of password, limit number of login attempts, inactive session logout, screen lock, and denial of repeated or recycled use of the same password. Vendor shall not store passwords electronically or in hardcopy documentation in clear text unless media is physically protected.
11	Account auditing and logging	Vendor shall provide a system whereby account activity is logged and is auditable both from a management (policy) and operational (account use activity) perspective. Write log files to read-only media to prevent malicious modification.
12	Role-based access control (RBAC)	Limit the exposure to risk associated with unauthorized actions by assigning the least privileges corresponding to the assigned duty or function.
13	Single sign-on	Single sign-on shall be used with RBAC and a two-factor authentication.

(continued)

Table 7-1. (*continued*)

System Hardening Precaution	Rationale
14	Flaw notification and documentation from vendor	Vendor shall provide documentation of a written flaw remediation process and provide appropriate software updates and/or workarounds to mitigate all vulnerabilities associated with the flaw. The process shall be used to track progress of patches and fixes.
15	Malware detection and protection	Vendor shall disclose the existence of any known backdoor codes. Provide host-based malware detection scheme and verify adequate system performance for malware detection, quarantine (instead of delete) suspected infected files and provide an updating scheme for the signatures.
16	Network addressing and name resolution	DNS servers are susceptible to cyber exploits including spoofing, cache poisoning, and denial-of-service (DoS) attacks. Static addressing schemes should be used. Enable cache pollution prevention and restrict addresses that can query control system DNS servers to control system hosts.
17	Intelligent electronic devices (including remote terminal units, sensors, actuators and meters)	Provide physical and cyber security features including, authentication, encryption, access control, event and communication logging, monitoring, and alarm to protect the device and configuration computer from unauthorized modification
18	Modems	Dial-up and dedicated modems shall be prohibited.
19	Cellular technology	Prohibited.
20	WiMAX technology	Prohibited.
21	Microwave and satellite	Prohibited.
22	Wireless mesh networks	Prohibited.
23	WirelessHART and ZigBee technologies	MGN shall include standard security measures.
24	Radio-frequency identification (RFID)	Provide RFID documentation if any.
25	Manual override control	Provide a means for manual override through a lockable enclosure or locking functionality in the device itself.
26	Bluetooth and wireless technology	Verify physical communications channels are secured from physical intrusion and document that the range is limited to within the building perimeter.
27	Managing network devices	Provide a method for managing network devices and changing addressing schemes.
28	Network configuration management	Verify that network configuration management interface is secured.
29	Security zones communications	Provide secure network architecture where the higher security zones originate communication with lesser security zones.
30	Disconnection points	Document disconnection points between network partitions and provide method to isolate subnets.

I am including the following list of recommendations in the hopes that hospital and healthcare facility administrators take action to protect their networks and medical equipment from cyber-attack. If the only things you do are the following eight items, I estimate the hospital cyber-attack surface will be *reduced by 90 percent*. Of course, having security policies for the building control systems and medical equipment networks is useless if they are not followed and enforced. Cybersecurity policy should also be reviewed periodically to incorporate the current threat environment, system functionality, and required level of security.

Discontinue Remote Connections to the Medical Equipment Network

Granted, the hospital personnel and medical equipment vendors want to access the equipment from the comfort of their recliner at home. So does the hacker. I have yet to see a building that does *not* have remote access. I asked a building maintenance engineer once if his building controls had remote access. He said "No." I asked to see his network diagram. I pointed to a box on the diagram marked Modem. "What's this?" I asked. He replied, "Oh, that's only used occasionally by the vendor for diagnostics." Obviously, we had it removed.

Implement Application Whitelisting

Application whitelisting can *detect* and *prevent* malware from executing. Networked medical devices are typically static systems that rarely change, so they are ideal for this defense. Application whitelisting is more effective than antivirus software because antivirus is not 100 percent effective.

■ **Application Whitelist**   A list or register of entities that are being provided a particular privilege, service, mobility, access, or recognition. Entities on the list will be accepted, approved, and/or recognized. Whitelisting is the reverse of blacklisting, the practice of identifying entities that are denied, unrecognized, or ostracized.

Systematic Patch Management Regimen

Just like burglars look for unlocked doors, hackers look for unpatched systems. Start with an asset inventory and baseline to track needed patches. Effective software patch management includes receiving updates on newly available patches, ensuring software patches are installed properly, testing systems after installation, and documenting all associated procedures. Ensure that software patches are imported from a safe, known source (hackers create a "watering hole" website so unsuspecting staff could download an infected version of the patch) and the patch is implemented quickly upon release. Don't forget to scan and patch PC-based laptops used to patch the equipment. Only known-good hospital laptops should connect to patch equipment and they should be stored securely at all times.

Reduce the Attack Surface

The medical equipment network should not connect to any other networks, especially the Internet. Lock down all unused ports. Turn off all unused services. Only allow real-time connectivity to external networks if there is a legitimate requirement. If one-way communication can accomplish a task, use optical separation (data diode). If bidirectional communication is necessary, then use a single open port over a restricted network path.

Build a Defendable Network Environment

Segment networks into logical enclaves and restrict host-to-host communications paths. This prevents hackers from expanding their access, while allowing normal system communications. Enclaving limits possible spread of malware and makes incident cleanup much faster and less costly. Consider using approved media instead of a network connection when transferring data from a secure network to a less secure network. Install perimeter devices on the network with access control lists such as firewalls or proxy servers. It can be enabled on the host via host-based firewalls and antivirus software.

Manage Authentication

Hackers are increasing attempting to obtain legitimate credentials, especially those with highly privileged accounts allowing them to masquerade as legitimate users. Implement three-factor authentication where possible (something you know, something you have, and something you are). Reduce privileges to only what's needed. Implement secure passwords (14 characters) for all accounts and change all passwords at least every 90 days. Require separate credentials for separate networks and zones.

Monitor and Respond

Watch IP traffic[3] for abnormal or suspicious communications; watch IP traffic within the medical equipment network for malicious connections or content; use host-based products to detect malicious software; use login analysis (time and place for example) to detect stolen credential usage or improper access, verifying all anomalies with quick phone call; watch account/user administration actions to detect control manipulation.

Do Not Use Medical Equipment Networks for Anything Else

Resist the temptation to use the medical equipment network for any other purpose. Do not allow a connection to check personal email, download software updates, surf the web or play computer games. The workstation should not even be connected to the enterprise network. That's how hackers get in. Exercise good personal cyber-hygiene.

Cybersecurity Analysis Tools

To ensure that the building is cyber-secure, an analysis should be performed using the DHS Cyber Security Evaluation Tool (CSET version 6.2). CSET is a self-contained software package developed under the direction of DHS Industrial Control System Cyber Emergency Response Team (ICS-CERT) by cybersecurity experts. CSET allows users to assess their controls and network security practices against industry standards. CSET runs on a desktop computer and makes recommendations for improvement of BCS cybersecurity.

---

[3]IP=Internet Protocol

Another DHS tool, the Cyber Resilience Review (CRR version 7) should also be used to evaluate the cybersecurity practices and assess risk incident management, service continuity, asset management, vulnerability, configuration, external dependency, and situational awareness. CRR uses a question and answer format to look at people, information technology, and facilities to assess the root causes of vulnerabilities so they can be addressed. The CRR examines policies and procedures, IT planning and management, IT infrastructure, IT operations, business operations, business continuity, disaster recovery, and risk management.

The CSET and the CRR Self-Assessment Package examine two different aspects of cybersecurity. The CSET software is a planning tool that describes the BCS hardware and software required to achieve a pre-determined Security Assurance Level (SAL). CSET produces a final Site Cyber Security Plan with a prioritized list of hardware and software recommendations to improve cybersecurity. The CRR is used as a self-assessment tool examining the BCS operational procedures of a fully operational facility.

Several computer simulations should be run with the CSET software package. The evaluation begins by the user designating a SAL based on the potential impact should a breach occur. The security categories for different information types are low, moderate, or high. The potential impact is "low" if the loss of confidentiality, integrity, or availability could be expected to have a limited adverse effect on the organization. A potential impact that is "moderate" is defined as a serious adverse effect on the organization, and "high" represents a severe or catastrophic adverse effect. Based on the security category selected, CSET generates a list of activities required to achieve the designated security categorization.

The following 44 items are MGN requirements for a hospital to achieve a "very high" SAL:

- MGN requires multifactor authentication for network access to privileged accounts.

- MGN monitors for unauthorized remote connections to the information system and takes appropriate action if an unauthorized connection is discovered.

- MGN encrypts passwords in storage and in transmission.

- MGN protects audit information and audit tools from unauthorized access, modification, and deletion.

- MGN uses PKI-based[4] authentication to validate certificates by constructing a certification path with status information to an accepted trust anchor; enforces authorized access to the corresponding private key; and maps the authenticated identity to the user account.

- MGN obscures feedback of authentication information during the authentication process to protect the information from possible exploitation/use by unauthorized individuals.

- MGN prevents non-privileged users from circumventing malicious code protection capabilities.

- MGN includes components specifically designed to be the target of malicious attacks for the purpose of detecting, deflecting, and analyzing cyber-attacks.

- MGN scans for vulnerabilities in the network and hosted applications.

- MGN employs vulnerability scanning tools and techniques that promote interoperability among tools and automates parts of the vulnerability management process.

- MGN employs malicious code protection mechanisms at network system entry and exit points and at workstations; and servers on the network to detect and eradicate malicious code.

---

[4]PKI=Public Key Infrastructure

- MGN monitors events on the network and devices and detects cyber-attacks.

- MGN provides near real-time alerts when indications of compromise or potential compromise occur.

- MGN detects unauthorized changes to software and information.

- MGN prevents the installation of unauthorized software programs.

- MGN monitors inbound and outbound communications for unusual or unauthorized activities.

- MGN prohibits the direct connection of the BCS network to an external network.

- MGN fails securely in the event of an operational failure of a boundary protection device.

- MGN blocks both inbound and outbound traffic between instant messaging clients.

- MGN employs virtualization techniques to present BCS components as other types of components, or components with differing configurations.

- MGN isolates security functions from non-security functions.

- MGN verifies the correct operation of security functions.

- MGN provides notification of failed automated security tests.

- MGN employs a wireless intrusion detection system to identify rogue wireless devices and to detect cyber-attack attempts and potential compromises/breaches.

- An effective MGN network device (e.g., routers, switches, firewalls) control program is implemented and includes instructions for restart and recovery procedures; restrictions on source code access, system utility access, and system documentation; protection from deletion of system and application files, and a structured process for implementation of directed solutions.

- Use of internal or external modems or wireless devices on the MGN is prohibited.

- MGN prevents the presentation of network system management-related functionality at an interface for non-privileged users.

- MGN prevents discovery of specific system components composing a managed interface.

- MGN enforces adherence to protocol formats.

- MGN manages excess capacity, bandwidth, or other redundancy to limit the effects of information flooding denial-of-service attacks.

- MGN behaves in a predictable and documented manner that reflects organizational and system objectives when invalid inputs are received.

- MGN detects network services that have not been authorized or approved and discovers indicators of compromise.

- MGN performs security compliance checks on constituent system components prior to the establishment of an internal connection.

- MGN restricts the use of maintenance tools to authorized personnel only.

- MGN implements cryptographic mechanisms to detect unauthorized changes to software, firmware, and information.

- MGN, upon detection of a potential integrity violation, provides the capability to audit the event, and then generates an audit record and alerts user.

- MGN system security design incorporates best security practices such as single sign-on, PKE,[5] smart card and biometrics.

- MGN complies with DoD[6] ports, protocols, and services guidance; AIS[7] applications; and outsourced IT-based processes and platforms. IT identifies the network ports, protocols, and services that they plan to use as early in the life cycle as possible and notify hosting enclaves. Enclaves register all active ports, protocols, and services.

- An incident response plan exists that identifies the responsible computer network defense service provider, defines reportable incidents, outlines a standard operating procedure for incident response, provides for user training and establishes an incident response team. The plan is exercised at least annually.

- MGN employs NIST FIPS 140-2[8] validated cryptography (e.g., DoD PKI class 3 or 4 token) is used to implement encryption (e.g., AES, 3DES, DES, Skipjack), key exchange (e.g., FIPS 171), digital signature (e.g., DSA, RSA, ECDSA), and hash (e.g., SHA-1, SHA-256, SHA-384, SHA-512).

- MGN establishes and manages cryptographic keys for the information system.

- MGN maintains availability of information in the event of the loss of cryptographic keys.

- MGN prevents unauthorized disclosure of information at rest and during transmission.

- MGN recognizes changes to information at rest and during transmission.

How to Avoid Phishing Scams

Hackers send millions of phishing emails every day. Many are obviously phony, but enough of them are convincing enough to fool some hospital employees. You should suspect emails with obvious spelling errors or very poor grammar. The following are words or phrases that hint that an email may be a phishing scam:

- "verify your account"

- "If you don't respond in 24 hours, your account will be closed"

- "Dear Valued Customer"

- "Click the link below to gain access to your account"

- "... attached ZIP file contains sensitive information from an attorney"

- "MAILER-DAEMON email delivery failure notification"

---

[5]PKE=public key cryptography
[6]U.S. Department of Defense
[7]AIS=application interface specification
[8]NIST=National Institute of Standards and Technology, FIPS=Federal Information Processing Standards

- "Your federal tax payment is available for refund"
- "Enter your Debit/Credit Card details ... get refund on your card"
- "Click to download your invoice"
- "Foreign lottery winnings"
- "Request your input for Survey on ..."
- "Work from home"
- "Naked picture of ...."
- "Sick Baby Donate"
- "When are you free to talk?"

Forged websites are the second-most popular phishing-scam attack vectors.

■ ■ ■

CHAPTER 8

Cyber-Attack Response and Recovery Planning

Unless you take the necessary precautions now, eventually your hospital will be the target of a cyber-attack. As I stated before, it is possible to reduce the damage potential by reducing the number of attack vectors. It is possible for a cyber-physical attack to be detected quickly thereby permitting equipment to shut down gracefully (before anyone is injured). The next step is rapidly restoring hospital systems and equipment to normal operation.

This begins with a well-thought-out Response and Recovery Plan so that when an attack occurs, you can make decisions quickly and take proper action to mitigate the damage. When a cyber-attack occurs, *the last thing you want to do is make things up as you go*. Taking the right steps ahead of time, and equipping your employees with the knowledge and tools they need to prevent an attack and deal with one when it occurs may save lives.

Although not written specifically for hospitals, my other book, *Cyber-Physical Attack Recovery Procedures* (Apress, 2016), is a *template* for *you* to modify based on the specific equipment in your hospital with instructions on how to restore building equipment to normal operation when systems begin to act erratically, or fail completely. When hackers shut off the hospital's electricity and water, disable the sewage effluent pumps, and activate the fire alarm, you have to do something quick. You won't have time to figure out the proper sequence of operations for your boilers and chillers. You need to quickly turn things off before a hacker can do any more damage. And, hackers can damage multiple systems in multiple buildings at the same time. That book can help you create custom checklists for your equipment.

Developing a Response and Recovery Plan

Preparing a Response and Recovery Plan satisfies the immediate need of having a documented plan; however, this is not enough if the goal is to have a viable response, resumption, recovery, and restoration capability. The Response and Recovery Plan and the activities associated with their maintenance (i.e., training, revision, and exercising) must become an integral part of hospital operations.

A Response and Recovery Plan is not a one-time document with a fixed start and end date. It should be an ongoing, properly funded (at least five percent of the annual IT budget) security activity intended to provide required resources to do the following:

- Perform activities required to construct recovery and restoration plans

- Train and retrain employees

- Develop policies and standards as the cyber-threat environment evolves

- Exercise strategies, procedures, team, and resources requirements

- Re-exercise unattained exercise objectives

© Luis Ayala 2016
L. Ayala, *Cybersecurity for Hospitals and Healthcare Facilities*, DOI 10.1007/978-1-4842-2155-6_8

- Report ongoing continuity planning to senior management

- Research processes and technologies to improve efficiency

- Perform plan maintenance activities

Developing Recovery Procedures that encompass activities required to maintain a viable continuity capability require a consistent planning methodology. The following are the Response and Recovery Plan elements necessary to create a viable, repeatable, and verifiable continuity capability:

- Implementing accurate and continuous vital records, data backup, and off-site data storage

- Implementing capabilities for rapid disconnect of communication circuits

- Providing alternate manual controls for equipment operations

- Constructing a contingency organization

- Implementing contingency strategies

Incident Response Teams

In the event of a cyber-physical attack, the normal organization of the hospital shifts into that of a contingency organization. The focus of the IT department, facility maintenance, and biomedical technicians shifts from "business as usual" to a concentrated team working toward the resumption of normal hospital operations. The hospital's facility maintenance staff, medical equipment vendors, IT staff, and security personnel participate in Incident Response Teams (IRT) through the phases of detection, mitigation, and recovery. Each phase requires the teams executing those procedures to work together closely. Each of the teams is comprised of individuals with specific responsibilities, which must be completed to fully execute the Response and Recovery Plan. There should be at least four teams: the Facilities Team, the Tech Support (IT) Team, Medical Equipment Team, and the Security Team. Primary and alternate team leaders are named during the preparation of the Response and Recovery Plan.

Each team becomes a subunit of the hospital's contingency organization and the teams are structured to provide dedicated, focused support in the areas of their particular experience and expertise for specific response, resumption and recovery tasks, responsibilities, and objectives. Each team's eventual goal is the resumption/recovery and the return to stable and normal hospital operations. Status and progress updates are reported by each team leader to hospital administration.

The following are the Incident Recovery Team's primary duties:

- To protect employees and equipment until normal hospital operations are resumed.

- To ensure that a viable capability exists to respond to a cyber-physical attack.

- To manage all response, resumption, recovery, and restoration activities.

- To support and communicate with hospital employees, system administrators, security officers, medical staff, and patients.

- To accomplish rapid and efficient resumption of hospital operations, technology, and functional support areas.

- To ensure that regulatory requirements are satisfied.

- To exercise resumption and recovery expenditure decisions.

- To streamline the reporting of resumption and recovery progress between the teams and management of each system.

Recovery Phases

A Recovery Procedures Coordinator, in conjunction with hospital management, determines which teams/team members are responsible for each function during each phase. As tasking is assigned, additional responsibilities, teams, and task lists may be prepared to address specific functions during a specific phase. Recovery after a cyber-attack can be described as three phases: detection, mitigation, and recovery.

Phase 1: Detection

- When anomalous behavior is observed such as multiple equipment failures, or a catastrophic event occurs, Intrusion Detection System alerts are sounded, the Incident Response Team consults an event diagnostics table[1] to determine if the "event" is a possible cyber-physical attack.

- The Incident Response Team then consults the integrity checks table to verify if a cyber-physical attack is underway.

- The Recovery Procedures Coordinator provides hospital management with the facts necessary to make informed decisions regarding subsequent resumption and recovery activity.

Phase 2: Mitigation

- The Incident Response Team's first priority is to isolate any compromised devices and protect the hospital facility and personnel through segmentation. The segmentation must be based on a predetermined strategy taking into account specific building equipment and medical equipment exigencies. After this step is complete, the Incident Response Team ensures that local network control has been achieved.

- The facility's Incident Response Team conducts a preliminary assessment of incident impact, extent of damage, known injuries, and disruption to the hospital operations and medical services.

- The Incident Response Team informs the Recovery Procedures Coordinator who determines if or when access to the hospital is allowed.

- The Recovery Procedures Coordinator establishes and organizes a management control center and headquarters for the recovery operations.

- The Recovery Procedures Coordinator implements procedures necessary to mobilize operations, support and department relocation as well as employee and external individuals and organizations notification before, during, and after recovery.

- The Recovery Procedures Coordinator notifies and appraises hospital administration of the situation.

---

[1]Detailed cyber-event diagnostics and integrity checks are beyond the scope of this book. Examples of these and other tables, forms, and checklists are found in my other book, *Cyber-Physical Attack Recovery Procedures*.

Phase 3: Recovery

- The Incident Response Teams execute investigations, incident response plans, and various other overarching command guidelines prior to executing any Recovery actions. They implement procedures necessary to facilitate and support the recovery of hospital operations.

- The Recovery Phase begins once the system under attack has been stabilized and infected equipment has been isolated from the controls networks. Replacement of infected devices with off-the-shelf replacements ensures that recovered devices are uncontaminated when reintegrated into the network and will aid in preservation of forensic evidence of the cyber-attack.

- The Incident Response Teams coordinate with employees, medical equipment vendors, and other internal and external stakeholders.

The After Action Report

After the network and all systems and services have been restored, an after-action report should be prepared. The After Action Report should include a complete description of the incident including how it was discovered, how systems were restored, lessons learned, and areas for improvement. It is the responsibility of each member of the Incident Response Team to reflect on the analyses and recommendations, determine which vulnerabilities may have applied to their areas of responsibility, and develop their own improvement plans and corrective actions. The Incident Response Team will share improvement plans and specify corrective actions for the hospital to take to prevent future cyber-attacks and mitigate their impact on hospital operations.

It is important to remember that a cyber-attack against a hospital is a *crime* that *must* be reported to law enforcement. It is the responsibility of the hospital administration to preserve *evidence* (including the proper chain of custody) to facilitate capture and prosecution of the criminals responsible, regardless where in the world they are located. A normal computer shutdown may cause valuable evidence to be erased, so you may want to simply pull the power plug; however, this is also risky. So, I recommend that you follow your IT department policies and recommendations.

CHAPTER 9

Appendix. Cyber-Attack Response Procedures Template

A soft copy of these forms (fully editable with fillable fields) is available for download from www.apress. com/9781484221549.

<<Facility Name>>
   <<Date Prepared>>
   <<Approved by: _____>>
   <<Date:_____>>

© Luis Ayala 2016
L. Ayala, *Cybersecurity for Hospitals and Healthcare Facilities*, DOI 10.1007/978-1-4842-2155-6_9

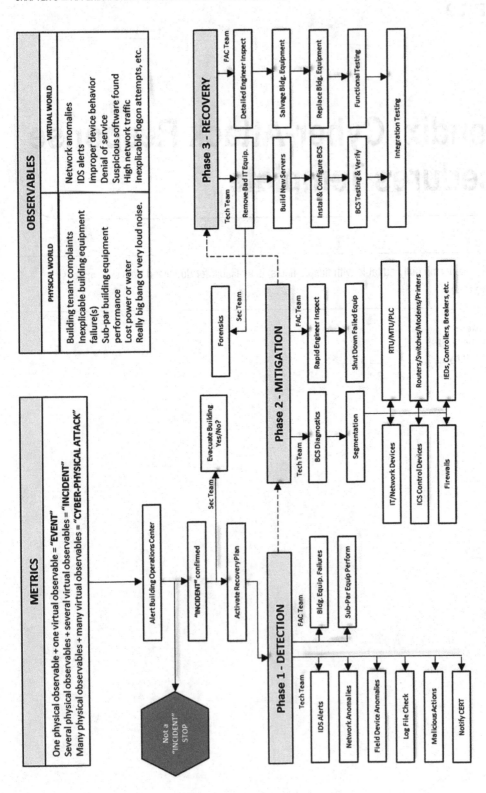

Figure 9-1. Cyber-Attack Response Procedures Flow Chart

Hospital Cyber-Attack Response Procedures

The following forms can be downloaded and customized to create your own Cyber-Attack Response Plan. Each form includes a brief description of the form, why the form is needed, who should fill out the form, and how often the form should be updated.

Intrusion Detection System Alerts

An intrusion detection system (IDS) is a hardware or software product that gathers and analyzes information from various areas within a computer network to identify possible security breaches, which include both intrusions (attacks from outside the organizations) and misuse (attacks from within the organizations.)

An IDS alerts us whenever it detects suspicious behavior such as any of the following:

- Unauthorized user logging in

- Virus or Trojan horse detected

- Rapid and/or continuous logins/logouts

- Users logging into accounts outside of normal working hours

- Numerous failed login attempts

- User accounts attempting to escalate account privileges

- Suspicious software and/or configurations on a server or workstation

- Unusual system behavior

- Irregular process found

- Spontaneous reboots or screen saver change

- Unusually slow performance or usually active CPU

- CPU cycles up and cycles down for no apparent reason

- Intermittent loss of mouse or keyboard

- Configuration files changed without user or system administrator action in operating system

- Configuration changes to software made without user or system administrator action

- Network unresponsive

- When an asset is communicating outside the bounds of the data flow baseline

- HMI, OPC, and controllers not synchronized

- Unexpected changes to instructions, function calls, commands, or alarm thresholds being sent from HMI or OPC to controllers

- HMI or OPC not updating after operator made changes to instructions, commands, or alarm thresholds

- Expected changes to controllers are not appearing on controllers

81

- An irregular vendor patch coming from an external source, or unexpected source, to a device within the network

- A device on the network is communicating with an undocumented, unauthorized, or unknown IP address

- A device other than authorized devices is sending field controller traffic to a network device

- Traffic coming or going to an unknown device

- A field controller is communicating with an unknown device

- A medical device has expanded its communications to other devices within the network

As you can see, there are many "observables" that tell us something is going on that we need to explore. Many alerts are not malicious and may be due to authorized events or can otherwise be explained:

- Was maintenance performed on the equipment or a software update installed recently?

- Did the equipment simply malfunction?

- Did the equipment lose network connectivity (outside the hospital)?

- Was a new medical device installed?

- Was a medical device reconfigured? Was it reconfigured correctly?

- Other authorized events are causing excessive network traffic.

- Was an old process removed from the network?

- User error.

If a cyber-event is detected *and* it cannot be explained, then we are compelled to perform integrity checks on *every* server, workstation, router, network switch, firewall, controller, all printers, and peripherals.

When a cyber-event is detected and it may be a cyber-physical attack, a *cyber-event ticket* is created and the appropriate Hospital Incident Response Team is called upon to investigate.

Cybersecurity Contacts

Form Description	This form instructs employee who to notify when they discover a cyber-event has occurred or when they suspect an attack is underway.
Why it's needed	Hospital employees need to react quickly to minimize hazards to patients. The form identifies who to contact and the telephone number.
Who fills it out	The Hospital Security Office, IT Office, and Building Maintenance enter telephone numbers and post the information where hospital staff can see it.
How often updated	Form should always list current contact information.

Person discovering the cyber-event should call:	
Whom to Call	**Telephone Number**
IT Helpdesk	
Building Operations Office	
Security Office	
IT Support Office	
Whichever office is contacted first shall contact the other hospital offices.	

Cybersecurity Breach Reporting Form – Page 1

Form Description	This form is used to record a cyber-event that has occurred or when it is suspected an attack is underway.
Why it's needed	The form requests information that may be valuable to defeat the cyber-attack and for preparing after-action report as well as to identify lessons learned to improve response in future.
Who fills it out	The hospital staff that is first contacted requests the information from the caller and distributes to other offices using both email and telephone messages while being sure other appropriate backup personnel and designated managers are contacted.
How often updated	Form should be updated as new information is learned.

The office alerted of the cyber-event will log:	
Name of the caller	
Time of the call	
Contact information about the caller	
Caller physical location	
The nature of the cyber-event	
How was the cyber-event detected?	
What equipment or persons were involved?	
Location of equipment or persons involved	

Description of Breach (select all that apply):
[ ]Loss or theft of device or media (e.g., computer, laptop, external hard drive, thumb drive, CD, tape)
[ ]Internal system breach
[ ]Insider wrongdoing
[ ]External system breach (e.g., hacking)
[ ]Active medical device corrupted
[ ]Passive medical device corrupted
[ ]Inadvertent disclosure
[ ]Other (specify):

Cybersecurity Breach Reporting Form – Page 2

The staff member could possibly add the following:	
Is this event an Emergency?	
Are active medical devices affected?	
Has the Medical Staff been alerted?	
What is the severity of the potential impact?	
Were critical hospital building systems affected?	
Name of equipment being targeted, along with operating system, IP address, and location.	
IP address and any information about the origin of the attack.	

Incident Response Team Strategy Meeting Form

Form Description	This form is used to record how the Incident Response Team assesses the situation when a cyber-attack is underway.
Why it's needed	The form requests information for preparing after-action report as well as to identify lessons learned to improve response in future.
Who fills it out	The Incident Response Team Leader.
How often updated	Form should be updated as new information is learned.

Hospital Incident Response Team Initial Meeting/Discussion
Is the cyber-event real or perceived?
Is the cyber-event still in progress?
What equipment or system is threatened and how critical is it?
What is the impact on the hospital should the attack succeed? Minimal, serious, or critical?
Where is the equipment located physically and on the network?
Is the cyber-event inside the trusted network?
Is the response urgent?
Can the cyber-event be quickly contained?
Will the response alert the attacker and do we care?
What type of cyber-event is this?   virus, worm, intrusion, abuse, damage

Cyber-Event Diagnostics Table

Form Description	This form is used to record the observable events that led to discovery that a cyber-attack was underway.
Why it's needed	The form requests information for preparing after-action report as well as to identify lessons learned to improve response in future.
Who fills it out	The Incident Response Team Leader.
How often updated	Form should be updated as new information is learned.

Check	Anomalous Behavior Observables
☐	Unusually heavy hospital network traffic
☐	Out of disk space or significantly reduced free disk space
☐	Unusually high CPU usage
☐	Creation of new user accounts
☐	Attempted or actual use of administrator-level accounts
☐	Locked-out accounts
☐	Accounts in use when the hospital employee is not at work
☐	Cleared log files
☐	Full log files with an unusually large number of events
☐	Antivirus or IDS alerts
☐	Disabled antivirus software and other security controls
☐	Unexpected patch changes
☐	Active Medical Devices connecting to outside IP addresses
☐	Requests for information about the network (social engineering attempts)
☐	Unexpected changes in a medical device's configuration settings
☐	Unexpected system shutdowns
☐	Stoppage or displayed error messages on a web, database, or application server
☐	Unusually slow access to hosts on the hospital network
☐	Filenames containing unusual characters or new or unexpected files and directories

(continued)

Check	Anomalous Behavior Observables
☐	Auditing configuration changes logged on the host records, disabling auditing function
☐	A large number of bounced emails with suspicious content
☐	Unusual deviation from typical hospital network traffic flows
☐	Erratic hospital building equipment behavior, more than one active medical device exhibits the same anomalous behavior
☐	Any apparent override of safety, backup, or failover systems
☐	Equipment, servers, or hospital network traffic that has bursts of temporary high usage when the operational process itself is steady and predictable.
☐	Unknown or unusual traffic from corporate network to hospital computer network
☐	Unknown or unexpected firmware pulls or pushes
☐	Loss of building utilities (electricity, water, gas, sewer equipment failure)
☐	Large number of complaints from medical staff
☐	Failure of multiple types of medical or building devices simultaneously
☐	Very high energy usage
☐	Obviously erroneous readings in medical device displays

Integrity Check Table

Form Description	This form is used to record the action taken to verify the integrity of various pieces of equipment when a cyber-attack occurs.
Why it's needed	The form provides information for recommended action to validate the integrity of the network and for preparing after-action report as well as to identify lessons learned to improve response in future.
Who fills it out	The Incident Response Team Leader.
How often updated	Form should be updated as new information is learned.

Check	Device Integrity	Description
☐	Computer unresponsive	**BOOT** from Rescue CD, use tools to uncover problems.
☐	Software processes	**REVIEW** processes to identify malicious activity. Includes data base servers, control servers, HMIs, OPCs, master terminal units (MTUs), and engineering workstations.
☐	Log files	**REVIEW** database servers, HMIs, control server, engineering workstations, OPCs, MTUs, and firewall log files for anomalies.
☐	Registry	**IDENTIFY** changes and anomalies in the registry.
☐	Rootkit	**CHECK** devices for a rootkit.
☐	Network communications	**VERIFY** network communications to the expected communications based on baseline. **VERIFY** data flow and compare to baseline.
☐	Unauthorized user activity	**REVIEW** host log files for user account changes.
☐	Firewalls	**DETERMINE** if configuration files, access control lists, operating system have been modified. **REVIEW** log file for anomalies or if log files have been modified.
☐	Switches and routers	**DETERMINE** if startup configuration, running configuration, or operating system files have been modified.
☐	Controllers	**VERIFY** the operating system, configuration files, and firmware against baseline. Includes PLCs, intelligent electronic devices, and remote terminal units.
☐	IDS Alerts – Inbound ICS Protocol	**DETERMINE** if IDS configuration files, rules, operating system, firmware, or log files have been modified. **DETERMINE** if the communications coming from the originating IP address should be communicating with the destination device.
☐	Peripherals and other network devices	**DETERMINE** if device has configuration files and operating system files, and whether they have been modified.
☐	Active medical devices	**DETERMINE** if medical device has configuration files and operating system files, and whether they have been modified.

Hospital Building Inspection – Page 1

Form Description	This form is used to record the action taken to determine the extent of damage to the building when a cyber-attack has taken place.
Why it's needed	The form provides point of contact information and for preparing after-action report as well as to identify lessons learned to improve response in future.
Who fills it out	The Incident Response Team Leader.
How often updated	Form should be updated as new information is learned.

Who does the inspection?	Facilities engineers, architects, structural, mechanical and electrical engineers, security officer, safety officer, city or county building, health and fire inspectors.
What do they inspect?	General property inspection and collection of records and if necessary, information needed to repair or replace damaged equipment. A **rapid inspection** is followed by a detailed **engineering inspection**. Engineers will inspect building columns, walls, ceilings, roof, masonry, windows, and doors for obvious hazards. They will also inspect stairs and elevators for safety hazards. Stuck doors and sagging ceilings can be indicators of structural weakness.
Why are they doing the inspection?	To identify damage in the building and reduce or permanently eliminate future risk to lives and property. Inspectors will take photographs and document the damage for reporting purposes and planning building repairs.
When do they do the inspection?	Inspections are conducted immediately after the incident as soon as building is accessible and/or when allowed entry by local officials.
What is the result of the inspection?	Obtain the local permits, certificates of occupancy, and any other required documentation to demonstrate compliance with local building/zoning/ life safety regulations.
What if the building does not pass inspection?	Develop a project plan and obtain necessary funding and approvals for building restoration and repairs. If the building is a complete loss, develop a plan to replace the building.

Hospital Building Inspection – Page 2

Agency	Contact Information
City Building Department	
Dept. of Public Works	
Fire Department	
Emergency Management	
CERT	
FEMA	
Electric Utility Company	
Natural Gas Utility Company	
Water and Sewer Utility	

Other Hospital Equipment to Be Checked

Form Description	This form is used to record the action taken to determine the extent of damage to other systems when a cyber-attack has taken place.
Why it's needed	The form provides information on the condition of various systems for preparing a response and after-action report as well as to identify lessons learned to improve response in future.
Who fills it out	The Incident Response Team Leader.
How often updated	Form should be updated as new information is learned.

System	Description
Fire Detection System	
Parking Garage Controls System	
Traffic Barriers	
Elevators	
Fire Pumps	
Smoke Evac System	
Lighting Controls	
Security Systems	
Closed Circuit TV	
Access Control System	
Storm Drainage System	
Incinerators	
Fire Sprinkler System	
Domestic Hot Water System	
Cable TV System	
Public Address System	
Energy Recovery Systems	
Solar Energy System	
Medium Voltage Electrical Distribution System	

(*continued*)

System	Description
Low Voltage Electrical Distribution System	
Electric Power Monitoring System	
Duress Alarm Systems	
Sewerage Pump System	
Wastewater Pump System	
Storm Drainage Utilities	
Sanitary Sewerage Utilities	
Door Locking System	

Cyber Event Ticket

Form Description	This form is used to record the action taken for a cyber-event.
Why it's needed	The form provides point of contact, description of the malfunction, action taken to mitigate damage. Useful for preparing after-action report as well as to identify lessons learned to improve response in future.
Who fills it out	The Incident Response Team member responding to the call.
How often updated	Form should be updated as new information is learned.

Cyber Event #:	Hospital Work Order #:
Work Order Type:	Customer Ref #:
Report Date:	Work Order Status:
Building:	Asset Worked On:

Additional Location Information:

Customer Request:

Conditions Found:

Actions Taken:

Date:	Status:			Date:	
	Technician Name	Start Time	Stop Time	Regular Hours	OT Hours

Part #	Description		Quantity	Unit Cost	Total Cost

Supply Rep Name	Technician Name/ Date Received	Supervisor Approval for High Value Items

Customer Signature & Date Completed	Customer Rating
x	
Technician Signature & Date Completed	**Customer Comment**
x	
QC Inspector Signature & Date Completed	**QC Comment**
x	

Event Category. Event will be categorized into the highest applicable level of one of the following categories (pick one):

Event Category	Description
One	An immediate threat to patient life/safety, hospital staff, or the public
Two	An immediate threat to critical hospital buildings or utilities
Three	A threat to hospital computer systems
Four	A minor disruption of hospital services

Equipment or Service Failure Report

Form Description	This form is used to describe the equipment that failed.
Why it's needed	The form provides a description of the malfunction discovered and the extent of repairs. Useful for preparing after-action report as well as to identify lessons learned to improve response in future.
Who fills it out	The Incident Response Team member responding to the call.
How often updated	Form should be updated as new information is learned.

Building:		Date:	Report No.:	
Area affected and phenomenon or condition failure:		Partial Failure ☐	Complete Failure ☐	
Mode of Discovery:	Alarm ☐	Rounds/ Inspection ☐	Abnormal Equipment Operation ☐	Medical Staff Complaint ☐	Preventive Maintenance ☒
Description of equipment or services that failed:					
Emergency or temporary measures and containment actions:					
Final or subsequent repairs:					
Repaired by:					
Defect: Open ☐ Closed ☐					

Remedial Action Required:
Yes ☐ No ☐
Describe:

Hospital personnel on duty at time of incident:	
Findings and Conclusions:	
Was this a cyber-attack?	

Explain:

Is the area safe for patients, hospital employees, or vendors?
Can equipment under examination function, and if so, at what percent of normal capacity?
What must be done to recover damaged equipment?
How long will it take to repair or replace the damaged equipment?

Using the damage assessment, determine the estimated time to recover based on the following guidelines:

- **Level I: Minimal damage** to hospital facility and/or medical devices. Estimated time to complete repairs is less than 4 hours.

- **Level II: Moderate damage** to hospital facility and/or medical devices. Estimated time to complete repairs is between 4 hours and 2 business days.

- **Level III: Extensive damage** to hospital facility and/or medical devices. Estimated time to complete repairs is greater than 2 business days.

☐	Identify equipment or spare parts that are immediately salvageable or in need of repair.
☐	Verbally notify the Hospital Administrator of survey results, assessment of damage, and rough estimate of time to recover.
☐	Document findings from the survey and damage assessment.
☐	Attend the recovery briefing to apprise Hospital Incident Recovery Team members of findings.
☐	A log is prepared and maintained to record all salvageable equipment and its disposition and location.

Hospital Incident Response Team Member Listing

Form Description	This form is used to identify individuals on the Incident Response Teams.
Why it's needed	The form provides a comprehensive list of Team members, their contact information, and when they were notified of the event.
Who fills it out	The Incident Response Team members provide information to Team Leader.
How often updated	Form should be updated as new information is learned.

Team Member Name	Cell Phone	Telephone	Time Called	E-mail
Management Team				
Leader				
Facilities Team				
Leader				
Tech Support Team				
Leader				
Security Team				
Leader				

This list should be filled out and kept current.

Repair Work Order Listing

Priority	Task Number	Summary	Estimated Completion Date

Recovery and Device Reintegration

Form Description	This form is used to identify which Incident Response Team does what.
Why it's needed	The form is a checklist listing the tasks needed to restore equipment, who performs the task, when they start the task and when the task is estimated to be complete.
Who fills it out	The Incident Response Team member provides information to Team Leader.
How often updated	Form should be updated as new information is learned.

Effective recovery after a cyber-attack requires ensuring that new reintegration devices will not be reinfected. The only way to avoid this problem is to verify that each device on the network is clean of any cyber-incident remnants. All devices in the network should be replaced or reflashed with known, good firm/software to provide confidence that reinfection will not occur.

Task	Prior	Description	IRT Team	Estimated Start	Estimated Finish
		RESTART undamaged equipment – manual control	FAC		
		PURCHASE new hospital facility equipment	FAC		
		INSTALL new hospital facility equipment	FAC		
		RUN new equipment – manual mode	FAC		
		RECEIVE new network equipment	Tech		
		INSTALL software from vendor CD-ROMs	Tech		
		INSTALL new servers	Tech		
		BOOT the servers	Tech		
		TEST operating system	Tech		
		TEST network	Tech		
		TEST medical devices	Tech		
		CONNECT hospital facility equipment to the BCS	MGMT/FAC/ Tech		
		TEST BCS with hospital facility equipment	MGMT/FAC/ Tech		
		ADVISE Hospital Administration	MGMT		

(continued)

101

Task	Prior	Description	IRT Team	Estimated Start	Estimated Finish
		REASSESS the situation	MGMT		
		SCHEDULE move dates for patient return	MGMT/FAC/Tech		
		ESTABLISH new building operating schedule	MGMT/FAC/Tech		
		MOVE patients back to hospital	MGMT		
		RESUME normal hospital operations	MGMT/FAC/Tech		
		MONITOR help desk for medical staff concerns	MGMT/FAC/Tech		
		PREPARE media statements	MGMT/SEC		
		PREPARE after-action report	MGMT/FAC/Tech		
		UPDATE Recovery Procedure w/Lessons Learned	MGMT/FAC/Tech		

Building Controls System Recovery and Reintegration

Form Description	This form lists recovery and reintegration tasks.
Why it's needed	The form is a checklist listing the tasks needed to restore equipment and the order in which they are to be completed.
Who fills it out	The Incident Response Team member provides information to Team Leader.
How often updated	Form should be updated as new information is learned.

The following Recovery and Reintegration checklists apply to all devices on the BCS network:

Servers

Workstations

Routers/Switches/Modems/Printers

Remote Terminal Units (RTU)/MTU/PLC

IEDs; Controllers, Breakers, Switches, Re-closers, Regulators

Human-Machine Interface (HMI)

Firewalls

Media Converters (Serial to Fiber, Serial to Ethernet)

	BCS Recovery
☐	**DOCUMENT** steps taken during recovery procedures for forensic analysis of the cyber-incident and possible use as evidence later on.
☐	**MAINTAIN** primary power (if possible) to the BCS device until an image can be saved of the onboard memory.
☐	**SAVE** an image of any hard drive(s) and volatile memory (if possible) for forensic analysis. This may require a reboot. **CAPTURE** volatile memory first, and then image the drive.
☐	**REMOVE and REPLACE** the affected BCS device.
☐	**DO NOT REIMAGE** any devices. Reimaging the affected device drive(s) will destroy forensic evidence of the cyber-incident.
☐	**VERIFY** the latest operating system, software, and firmware patches are installed on the device. **INSTALL** updates prior to reintegration in the BCS.
☐	**UPDATE** passwords on all BCS devices (including seldom-used obscure modules).
☐	**UPDATE** the antivirus software and intrusion detection software and **RUN** a full system scan.

(*continued*)

	BCS Reintegration
☐	**DO NOT RECONNECT** the device to other devices in the network until each device in the affected network layer or affected subsystem has been recovered per these procedures.
☐	**VERIFY** that each device in the isolated layer or subsystem has been properly recovered. **CONSULT** the cyber-incident records to confirm that *Recovery* has been performed on these devices prior to reintegration on the BCS network.
☐	When each device in the layer or subsystem has been properly recovered and documented, **RECONNECT** all of the devices.
☐	**DO NOT RECONNECT** to the enterprise network.
☐	**VERIFY** that the forensics specialists have eliminated cyber-incident artifacts using detection tools (IDS, Log Review, Nmap, Netstat, Wireshark, etc.) and documented the results.
☐	**MONITOR** the BCS for anomalous BEHAVIOR.
☐	If anomalous behavior is still evident, **REPEAT** the detection procedures and/or mitigation procedures as necessary.
☐	When the layer or subsystem is operating without evidence of the cyber-incident, and the Recovery Procedures Coordinator gives approval, **RECONNECT** the isolated layer or subsystem to the BCS.
☐	**MONITOR** the system for anomalous behavior.
☐	If anomalous behavior is still evident, **REPEAT** the detection procedures and/or mitigation procedures as necessary.
☐	**SUBMIT** all records of recovery actions to the Recovery Procedures Coordinator.
☐	**RETURN** to routine monitoring of the network.

■ **Customize**   the form for your specific hospital and verify the normal operating conditions when the recovery procedures are prepared.

Building Controls System Field Test

All point-to-point testing of end field devices through proper input/output to graphic and operator interface shall be completed and approved.

All field calibration shall be completed and approved.

Detailed functional tests shall verify that the system adheres to the sequence of operation.

All alarm limits shall be completed and approved.

All schedule start/stops and system setpoints shall be entered, operating and approved.

General: Adjust, calibrate, measure, program, configure, set the time schedules, and ensure that the systems function as specified in the sequence of operations.

Systems Check: An item-by-item check shall be performed for each HVAC system.

- **Step 1 – System Inspection:** With the system in unoccupied mode and with fan hand-off-auto switches in the OFF position, it shall be verified that power and main air are available where required and that all output devices are in their failsafe and normal positions. Each local display panel and each M&C Client shall be inspected to verify that all displays indicate shutdown conditions.

- **Step 2 – Calibration Accuracy Check:** A two-point accuracy check of the calibration of each HVAC control system sensing element and transmitter shall be performed by comparing the value from the test instrument to the corresponding SNVT. Digital indicating test instruments shall be used, such as digital thermometers, motor-driven psychrometers, and tachometers. The test instruments shall be at least twice as accurate as the specified sensor accuracy. The calibration of the test instruments shall be traceable to National Institute of Standards and Technology standards. The first checkpoint shall be with the HVAC system in unoccupied mode with fan hand-off-auto switches in the OFF position, and the second checkpoint shall be with the HVAC system in an operational condition. Calibration checks shall verify that the sensing element-to-DDC system readout accuracies at two points are within the specified product accuracy tolerances. If not, the device shall be recalibrated or replaced and the calibration check repeated.

- **Step 3 – Actuator Range Check:** With the system running, a signal shall be applied to each actuator through the DDC Hardware controller. Proper operation of the actuators and positioners for all actuated devices shall be verified and the signal levels shall be recorded for the extreme positions of each device. The signal shall be varied over its full range, and it shall be verified that the actuators travel from zero stroke to full stroke within the signal range. Where applicable, it shall be verified that all sequenced actuators move from zero stroke to full stroke in the proper direction, and move the connected device in the proper direction from one extreme position to the other.

Operational Security Log

Form Description	This form is used to identify physical security safeguards that were implemented by Team members.
Why it's needed	The form lists the equipment that needs to be safeguarded, when the equipment was secured and how it was secured. This will support the chain of custody for evidence later on as well as for the after action report.
Who fills it out	The Incident Response Team member provides information to Team Leader.
How often updated	Form should be updated as new information is learned.

Date: Time	Asset	Operator: IP Address	Description	Action Taken	Results

Medical Network Recovery and Device Reintegration

Form Description	This form lists recovery and reintegration tasks for medical grade network and medical devices.
Why it's needed	The form is a checklist listing the tasks needed to restore equipment and the order in which they are to be completed.
Who fills it out	The Incident Response Team member provides information to Team Leader.
How often updated	Form should be updated as new information is learned.

The following Recovery and Reintegration checklists apply to all devices on the networks:

Servers

Workstations

Routers/Switches/Modems/Printers

Remote Terminal Units (RTU)/MTU/PLC

IEDs; Controllers, Breakers, Switches, Re-closers, Regulators

Human-Machine Interface (HMI)

Firewalls

Media Converters (Serial to Fiber, Serial to Ethernet)

Medical Devices

	Network Recovery
☐	**DOCUMENT** steps taken during recovery procedures for forensic analysis of the cyber-incident and possible use as evidence later on.
☐	**MAINTAIN** primary power (if possible) to the medical device until an image can be saved of the onboard memory.
☐	**SAVE** an image of any hard drive(s) and volatile memory (if possible) for forensic analysis. This may require a reboot. **CAPTURE** volatile memory first, and then image the drive.
☐	**REMOVE** and **REPLACE** the affected device.
☐	**DO NOT REIMAGE** any medical devices. Reimaging the affected device drive(s) will destroy forensic evidence of the cyber-incident.
☐	**VERIFY** the latest operating system, software, and firmware patches are installed on the device. **INSTALL** updates prior to reintegration in the network.
☐	**UPDATE** passwords on all devices (including seldom used obscure modules).
☐	**UPDATE** the antivirus software and intrusion detection software and **RUN** a full system scan.

(continued)

Device Reintegration	
☐	**DO NOT RECONNECT** the device to other devices in the network until each device in the affected network layer or affected subsystem has been recovered per these procedures.
☐	**VERIFY** that each device in the isolated layer or subsystem has been properly recovered. **CONSULT** the cyber-incident records to confirm that *recovery* has been performed on these devices prior to reintegration on the hospital network.
☐	When each device in the layer or subsystem has been properly recovered and documented, **RECONNECT** all of the medical devices.
☐	**DO NOT RECONNECT** to the enterprise network.
☐	**VERIFY** that the forensics specialists have eliminated cyber-incident artifacts using detection tools (IDS, Log Review, Nmap, Netstat, Wireshark, etc.) and documented the results.
☐	**MONITOR** the network for anomalous **BEHAVIOR**.
☐	If anomalous behavior is still evident, **REPEAT** the detection procedures and/or mitigation procedures as necessary.
☐	When the layer or subsystem is operating without evidence of the cyber-incident, and the Recovery Procedures Coordinator gives approval, **RECONNECT** the isolated layer or subsystem to the network.
☐	**MONITOR** the system for anomalous behavior.
☐	If anomalous behavior is still evident, **REPEAT** the detection procedures and/or mitigation procedures as necessary.
☐	**SUBMIT** all records of recovery actions to the Hospital Recovery Procedures Coordinator.
☐	**RETURN** to routine monitoring of the network.

■ **Customize** form for your specific hospital and verify the normal operating conditions when the recovery procedures are prepared.

Hospital Data Network Information

Form Description	This form lists vital information for critical network equipment.
Why it's needed	The form is a checklist listing the information needed to restore equipment after a cyber-attack.
Who fills it out	The Incident Response Team members.
How often updated	Form should be updated as new information is learned.

Date Updated	
Unique Application ID	
Application Name	
Owner (e.g., department, etc.)	
Custodian (e.g., departmental IT staff, vendor)	
Description	
User Base/Scope	
Business Function	
Data Classification	
Criticality	
Date of Last Business Impact Analysis (BIA)	
Operating System	
Asset Tag	
Serial Number	
Licensing Information	
Vendor (or, internally developed)	
Maintenance Contract Expires	
Maintenance Contact	
Current Instances (e.g., production and test, test only, production only)	
Program Language (s)	
Internet Accessible	
Requires own server	

(*continued*)

Desktop Data Storage (e.g., what files/configuration are required if app allows or requires storage of data on workstations)	
External File Requirements	
Domain Information	
Service Account (s)	
Storage Requirements	
Seats/Units	
Load Balancing	
License Requirements	
Protocol Requirements	
Port Requirements	
Network Requirements	
IP Address/Range	
Minimum Client Requirements	
Encryption Requirements	
Third Party Requirements (e.g., applications or software required)	
Code Libraries	
Known Bottlenecks	
Batch Processing Details (e.g., scheduled tasks, duration, subtasks, etc.)	
Backup Software	
Backup Type	
Backup Frequency/Schedule	
Media	
Offsite Storage Location	
Generations Offsite	
Source Code Backed Up?	
Additional Details	
Maintenance Window Details	
Vendor /Internal contact information	

(*continued*)

Recovery Point Objective (RPO)	
Recovery Time Objective (RTO)	
Priority	
Additional Details	
Supporting Documentation Location	
Additional Details	
Application is dependent on the following hardware resources:	
Other processes dependent on this application:	
Applications/services dependent on this resource:	
Applications/services this resource is dependent on:	

This list should be filled out and kept current.

Building Controls System Network Information

Form Description	This form lists vital information for critical BCS network equipment.
Why it's needed	The form is a checklist listing the information needed to restore equipment after a cyber-attack.
Who fills it out	The Incident Response Team members.
How often updated	Form should be updated as new information is learned.

Date Updated	
Unique Application ID	
Application Name	
Owner (e.g., department, etc.)	
Custodian (e.g., departmental IT staff, vendor)	
Description	
User Base/Scope	
Business Function	
Data Classification	
Criticality	
Date of Last Business Impact Analysis (BIA)	
Operating System	
Asset Tag	
Serial Number	
Licensing Information	
Vendor (or, internally developed)	
Maintenance Contract Expires	
Maintenance Contact	
Current Instances (e.g., production and test, test only, production only)	
Program Language (s)	
Internet Accessible	
Requires own server	
Desktop Data Storage (e.g., what files/configuration are required if app allows or requires storage of data on workstations)	

(continued)

External File Requirements	
Domain Information	
Service Account (s)	
Storage Requirements	
Seats/Units	
Load Balancing	
License Requirements	
Protocol Requirements	
Port Requirements	
Network Requirements	
IP Address/Range	
Minimum Client Requirements	
Encryption Requirements	
Third Party Requirements (e.g., applications or software required)	
Code Libraries	
Known Bottlenecks	
Batch Processing Details (e.g., scheduled tasks, duration, subtasks, etc.)	
Backup Software	
Backup Type	
Backup Frequency/Schedule	
Media	
Offsite Storage Location	
Generations Offsite	
Source Code Backed Up?	
Additional Details	
Maintenance Window Details	
Vendor /Internal contact information	
Recovery Point Objective (RPO)	
Recovery Time Objective (RTO)	
Priority	

(*continued*)

Additional Details	
Supporting Documentation Location	
Additional Details	
Application is dependent on the following hardware resources:	
Other Processes dependent on this application:	
Applications/services etc. dependent on this resource:	
Applications/services etc. this resource is dependent on:	

This list should be filled out and kept current.

Medical Device and Equipment Vendor Contact List

Form Description	This form is used to identify equipment representatives.
Why it's needed	The form provides a comprehensive list of manufacturer's field maintenance personnel, their contact information so they can be notified of the event quickly.
Who fills it out	The Incident Response Team members.
How often updated	Form should be updated as new information is learned.

This is a listing of all vendors and contractors that currently provide support or will provide support in a post-disaster environment. Additionally, any service level agreements (SLAs) that have been executed and all subsequent modifications should be attached.

Vendor Contact List

Vendor	Equipment	Contact Name	Telephone	Email

List of Authorized Maintenance Laptop Computers

Form Description	This form is used to identify hospital laptop computers that are approved for use on the network.
Why it's needed	The form provides a comprehensive list of approved equipment including the date of the most recent virus scan.
Who fills it out	The Incident Response Team member provides information to Team Leader.
How often updated	Form should be updated as new information is learned.

The Authorized Maintenance Laptop List may be unique to each building and should be readily available to the IRT. The list includes the date of the last virus scan for each. Authorized maintenance laptops *must* be stored in a secure location and only issued to onsite vendors for use on site. When needed for more than one day, laptops shall be collected at the end of each day and locked away. Laptop shall be scanned for virus and malware prior to connection to the BCS every time. After use, vendor software shall be wiped and drive scanned prior to returning to storage.

Authorized Maintenance Laptop List	
Date of Last Virus Scan	Laptop Number

Vulnerability Assessments History

Form Description	This form identifies when the network was last scanned and the name of the company that performed the scan.
Why it's needed	The form includes brief recommendations made by the company that performed the scan.
Who fills it out	The Incident Response Team Leader.
How often updated	Form should be updated as new information is learned.

Types of Internal and External Vulnerability Tests
White-Box Test Team

Test team has complete access to the hospital network including network diagrams, hardware, operating system, and application details. Knowledge of hospital network allows targeting specific building equipment, applications, and active medical devices.

Gray-Box Test Team

Test team simulates attack by a disgruntled employee. Test team has user-level privileges and access permitted to the hospital network with certain security policies relaxed.

Black-Box Test Team

Test team has no prior knowledge of hospital network (except possibly a website URL or IP address). Test team attempts to break into the hospital network remotely.

Scan Date	Testing Team & Type	Company	Recommendations

Vulnerability Test Types

1. **External Vulnerability Scan**: Identify network-facing vulnerabilities (Monthly).

2. **Internal Vulnerability Scan**: Identify network-facing vulnerabilities (Quarterly).

3. **External Vulnerability Assessment**: Identify configuration and architecture vulnerabilities (Annual).

4. **Internal Vulnerability Assessment**: Identify network, client, configuration, and physical vulnerabilities (Annual).

5. **Penetration Test**: Exploit any vulnerability to obtain access to building controls (Annual).

Vulnerabilities Notifications Reports

Form Description	The following forms list the vulnerabilities that were announced for equipment that the hospital maintains, indicates when the vulnerability was announced, the impact of the vulnerability if not fixed, and when the patch was installed.
Why it's needed	The forms include a brief description of the vulnerability and the system affected.
Who fills it out	The Incident Response Team Leader.
How often updated	Form should be updated as new information is learned.

Hospital Data Network Vulnerabilities Notifications Report

This is a list of announced system vulnerabilities for the Hospital Data Network.

Announced Hospital Network Vulnerabilities					
Bulletin ID. or Name	Description	System Affected	Release Date	Resolved	Impact

Hospital Data Network Software Management Report

This is a list of installed and missing service packs on the Hospital Data Network.

Installed and Missing Service Packs

Bulletin ID. or Name	Description	System Affected	Release Date	Severity	Lab Test Date	Patch Date	Complete Pending	Name of Tester

Building Controls System Network Vulnerabilities Notifications Report

This is a list of announced system vulnerabilities for the Building Controls System.

Announced Hospital Network Vulnerabilities					
Bulletin ID. or Name	Description	System Affected	Release Date	Resolved	Impact

Building Controls System Network Software Management Report

This is a list of installed and missing service packs on the Building Controls System.

Installed and Missing Service Packs								
Bulletin ID. or Name	Description	System Affected	Release Date	Severity	Lab Test Date	Patch Date	Complete Pending	Name of Tester

Medical Device Data System Vulnerabilities Notifications Report

This is a list of announced system vulnerabilities for the Medical Device Data System.

Announced Hospital Network Vulnerabilities					
Bulletin ID. or Name	Description	System Affected	Release Date	Resolved	Impact

Medical Device Data System Software Management Report

Form Description	The form lists the software updates that were announced for equipment the hospital maintains.
Why it's needed	The form indicates when the software patch was available for each system, the impact of the vulnerability if not fixed, and when the patch was installed and tested and who conducted the test.
Who fills it out	The Incident Response Team Leader.
How often updated	Form should be updated as new information is learned.

This is a list of installed and missing service packs on the Medical-Grade Network.

Installed and Missing Service Packs

Bulletin ID. or Name	Description	System Affected	Release Date	Severity	Lab Test Date	Patch Date	Complete Pending	Name of Tester

Index

Get the eBook for only $5!

Why limit yourself?

Now you can take the weightless companion with you wherever you go and access your content on your PC, phone, tablet, or reader.

Since you've purchased this print book, we're happy to offer you the eBook in all 3 formats for just $5.

Convenient and fully searchable, the PDF version enables you to easily find and copy code—or perform examples by quickly toggling between instructions and applications. The MOBI format is ideal for your Kindle, while the ePUB can be utilized on a variety of mobile devices.

To learn more, go to www.apress.com/companion or contact support@apress.com.

Printed in the United States
By Bookmasters